Praise for

Turtle Wisdom has morphed, just as I have of itself over time. This beautifully written book called to me many years ago at a time when I knew I needed something but didn't know what it was. Its precious cover grabbed my attention away from any and all other books on the shelf. Donna DeNomme has a way of letting the reader feel like she is sitting right there with you, looking directly into your soul as she invites you to come back home to yourself. And this little Turtle ... she just keeps on giving.
~ Holyce McIntire, Compassionate Photography

Donna DeNomme is the real-life embodiment of Yoda. Whether you're navigating through layers of personal trauma or simply seeking to up-level your life, Donna's ancient wisdom teachings are like a flashlight illuminating a clear path forward. They lay before you the wisdom to awaken the insight, the potent power, personal empowerment, and the love you're seeking, and reveal "the force" that was there all the time. ~ Becky Swenson, Radiant Living Guide

Turtle Wisdom crosses many cultures and is a timeless representation of how to live life. It continues to be a bestseller as #1 in the self-help category. All I have to do is put a turtle next to it and it sells! *Turtle Wisdom* is pure food for the soul. What a perfect gift. ~ Dianne Fresquez, Owner of For Heaven's Sake Books

Breaking away from the glut of self-help books that follow the over-used 'how to' formulas, *Turtle Wisdom* takes you on a journey that leaves you feeling as if your favorite grandmother has wrapped you up in a cozy blanket, gently placed you by the fireplace with a cup of your favorite hot chocolate, and lovingly rocked you to sleep on a frigid winter night. ~ Tom LaRotanda, Corporate Coach, Speaker

This book has inspired me over and over again throughout my life. I want to gift this book to all who need a life preserver. I can't wait to be the one who throws it out to them. ~ Coleen Hampf, Teacher of small children, Grandmother

I read a few passages as I fall asleep so I can seed my dreams with powerful positive affirmations. I applaud Ms. DeNomme's intention to encourage us to live consciously and celebrate what we are!" ~ Caryn Colgan, *Ancient Pact*

Donna DeNomme is a master at distilling important advice into small bites that make sense and will make you want to take action to achieve self-acceptance and understanding. Just hang onto those turtles and follow the path to where they take you! ~ Tina Proctor, Wisdom circles for aging adults, Wanderer, Grandmother

I often pick up my *Turtle Wisdom* and just randomly open a page to fill my love bucket. ~ Barbara Vande Berg, M.Div., Vital Energy Master

Turtle Wisdom is a book that I plan to read every year because I know it will meet me where I am at. It is a gem of a road map for self-care. Thank you for your transparency and wisdom Donna—may we all discover our extraordinary potential within. ~ Sharon Barrett, Grandmother, Gardener, Botanical Illustrator

Turtle Wisdom is a wealth of powerful spiritual knowledge that is approachable and inspirational. The book offers practical guidance on changes you can make today to lead a more fulfilling and resilient life. It encourages you to take the lead in your life so that you can celebrate all that your precious life has to offer.
~ Elisa Brossard, Leadership Coach

I love that sweet, precious turtle! I reached out to Donna because I wanted many copies to give to my friends. Everyone should have a turtle to inspire their day. I try to live life to its fullest ... and just like the turtle I keep moving on.
~ Muriel, Retired but busy at 105 years young

Love, love, love this whole series! I found each one delightful to read and useful for a quick daily boost ... and as a personal and business coach, I often recommend *Turtle Wisdom* book, playbook, and cards to my clients.
~ Sherry Ray, *Finding Traction: Recapture Your Drive at Work*

Turtle Wisdom is a gem. Donna's wisdom and techniques will guide you on your way to cherishing the magnificent being you are.
~ Susyn Reeve, *Choose Peace and Happiness*

I have been on my own spiritual journey for more than 30 years. I have come to believe that most of what we as human beings suffer from, whether it is mental, physical or emotional, is that we have lost or forgotten our essential connection to the sacred in ourselves and in our everyday living. It is a "spiritual hunger" of great magnitude. Donna DeNomme's beautifully written and inspirational book not only calls us home to that place within, but also creates the path of getting there. ~ Lynda Barbaccia, *Simple Wisdom for the Not So Simple Business World*

Donna DeNomme's comfortable and comforting style of wisdom and humor helps the bruised Soul, tender from damage, find healing, strength and a way forward to Self. ~ Carridwen Brennan, Spiritual Counselor, Tri-State Prison Project

It is 4 am ... I haven't been to bed yet, rest can wait. My Soul/Spirit was thirsty like a sponge. I have read the whole book. I have been reading all night ... With new hope, renewed strength, and direction, I believe in me again! Thank you.
~ Mona Rose, Workshop Participant

This book grows with you. You can't read it too many times and you can't get enough. And those little turtles make me smile! ~ Toni Grishman, BSN, RN

This is a simple and elegant prescription for living. It's thoroughly enjoyable and entertaining, with practical advice and suggestions for letting go of the past and truly living your life in the present.
~ Dr. Steven Farmer, Best-selling Author of *Earth Magic* and *Animal Spirit*

If you crave the comfort, love, and guidance that's like a friend or sister whom you can curl up with, grab a cup of tea and snuggle up with *Turtle Wisdom*.
~ Laya Saul, *You Don't Have to Learn Everything the Hard Way*

Donna DeNomme is a gifted writer and powerful spiritual practitioner, bringing commitment, creativity and powerful spiritual passion. Her compassion and connection with Spirit make her a tremendous blessing.
~ Dr. Roger Teel, *This Life is Joy*

Turtle Wisdom is a delightful pocket-guide for living a rich life!
~ Dr. Deborah Sandella, PhD, RN, *Releasing the Inner Magician*

It's obvious Donna has walked the long walk of learning how to love herself.
~ Tama J. Kieves, *This Time I Dance! Creating the Work You Love*

Your book has left me feeling as if I've had an emotional massage, as if I'm in a private session with you, wrapped in love and safety. The illustrations add a sweetness ... My heart is so full of joy! ~ Judith Lynne, Author

Donna's insights have the power to bring more joy to your life. Open up your heart, open up this book, and take it all in.
~ Jana Stanfield, Keynote Speaker, Singer and Songwriter

Donna DeNomme reminds us, in a gentle and practical way, that we have within us the essence of the Divine. By following her clear suggestions, anyone seeking to grow into his/her own spiritual skin can methodically peel away the dust of life to reveal the power, beauty, and wisdom resting in the soul.
~ Susan Schachterle, *What Would You Do If You Knew You Couldn't Fail?*

I have spent decades seeking safety and in just a few words, Donna has spoken truth in simplicity ... *Turtle Wisdom* blesses the world!
~ Rev. Nadine Cox, CSL, Artist, *How to Give Your Power Away and How to Reclaim It*

Thank you, Donna, for your incredibly intuitive cards and reading material that has helped me to process and grow as a more loving person in this world. You truly bring us closer to our authentic selves. May your future endeavors help us all be better beings. ~ Victoria Atwell, Massage Therapist

Turtle Wisdom

Coming Home to Yourself

A Delightful Companion for Living a Happy, Authentic Life

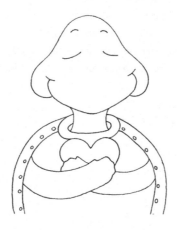

Donna DeNomme

Illustrations by Sue Lion

ISBN 978-0-9848589-2-7
Library of Congress Control Number: 2023946232
All rights reserved. Printed in Canada.
No part of this publication may be reproduced, stored in a retrieval system
or transmitted in any form or by any means, electronic, mechanical, photocopying,
recording, or otherwise, without the written permission of the publisher.

Your Wisdom Story Publishing
18719 W. 60th Avenue, Golden, Colorado 80403
donna@yourwisdomstory.com
www.YourWisdomStory.com
Copyright © 2023. All Rights Reserved. Your Wisdom Story Publishing

Portrait photograph: Steve Kindsfather
Cover design: Susan Andra Lion, www.suelion.com
Book design and Illustrations: Susan Andra Lion

1. Motivational. 2. Inspirational. 3. Personal Growth. 4. Transformational Activities.

Table of Contents

Preface: Coming Home to Yourself ... xi

Section 1

1. The Golden Opportunity is Within You ... 1
2. Sitting with Yourself ... 7
3. No One Else Can Do It! ... 21
4. How Does Your Garden Grow? Cultivating a Truer You ... 27

Section 2

5. Coming of Age: Recognizing All That You Are ... 67
6. In the Moment ... 85
7. I'm Stuck with Me! ... 105
8. Difficult Days ... 127
9. The Alchemy of Your Troubles ... 157

Section 3

10. Your Body, Your Temple ... 173
11. Exposing Your Soft Belly ... 183
12. Turtle Wisdom: She Who Holds Up the World ... 203
13. Open to Possibilities ... 219

Postscript: You Write the Final Chapter(s) ... 229

Author Notes and Biographies ... 231

Whoever you are,

Wherever you are,

Whatever is going on in your life,

This is the call ...

come home ...

to yourself.

Preface

Coming Home to Yourself

*This above all
to thine own self be true.*

~ William Shakespeare

Years ago, the axis of my world tilted. I found myself gradually running out of steam, until one day I was so tired that it became a great mental and physical effort simply to walk across the room. My work suffered, my house was a disaster, but even worse was that I did not have the least bit of energy to feel happiness or joy, or any emotion for that matter. I was just too tired to feel. There was this sort of flatline emotionally that sucked every ounce of good out of my days. The natural act of thinking was overwhelming; the arduous slow-turning mental function took an extended period and sometimes didn't even make any sense. Later, during moments of clarity, I would realize that there was a simple answer that my brain simply could not access at the time it was needed. I would have been frustrated if I could have spared the energy!

With the help of my acupuncturist and my primary physician, I was able to re-balance my metabolism. It was fascinating to observe my brain function as it gradually returned. I was impressed by how many activities I could juggle at the same time without effort. My brain simply handled this and that and the other thing, without the tedious pushing I had now become accustomed to exerting—to experience this change so dramatically deepened my admiration for the human mind (and for myself).

I had almost lost me … at least my sense of me. The "me" I could always depend on. The capable, get it done me. Just getting through the day had been a chore. I went to bed exhausted and woke exhausted, too. Yet, it was during this desperate time that the concept of "appreciating myself" fully developed. The roots of this understanding had formed much earlier.

When I was very young, my family entrusted me to people who were supposed to care for me. Instead, they hurt me in ways that weren't visible to the naked eye; yet these wounds ached and burned to the touch until I was well into my forties. Unbeknownst to my parents, I had been terrorized for several years through physical, mental, sexual, and even psychic abuse. Although my abusers had free reign over me, having me captive six days a week, they were never able to penetrate and destroy my innermost core. Despite all that was done to me, my spirit was not broken and what was essential remained intact.

And, in fact, for some peculiar reason, this horrific experience turned out to be a powerful catalyst for me, not only for my own healing, but in determining the life work I would pursue. The harshness I was subjected to caused me to reach deeply within myself and access a much-needed, sustainable inner strength. There was something unshakable and absolute that remained whole despite the fractured reality of my outer circumstance. There was a thread of comfort right there, inside of me, right in the midst of my feeling abandoned and alone.

> When a catastrophe hits, we are left to deal with the aftermath. Perhaps a life challenge or health crisis alters our outer reality or somehow changes us; yet always, we possess our own precious inner Core Essence. **What is essential is still intact;** what is essential never leaves or can be taken away. It remains somewhere within you, waiting for you to reach your hand out to beckon it forward.
>
> Between insecurity and vulnerability, you can find a deeper level of assurance and trust—an assurance in yourself and a trust in life itself having an innate, enduring force that moves toward the good. You discover that you can draw on your own inner resources which remain dependably consistent and whole.
>
> As you navigate through change or adapt to a new way of being, cultivate an expanded appreciation of yourself as you draw from those resilient inner resources. Just lean in ... and discover the gifts that are buried there. Move through step-by-step, ultimately trusting the path you have been placed upon.

When I was experiencing the thyroid shift, I tried to ride the wave, doing tasks when I had energy, and sitting when I did not. It was interesting that on days when I could not physically handle much, I could still garden for hours and sometimes write. It was as if my soul longed for these creative ventures and would force me in those directions by taking away my work-worthiness. It was during this time of challenge that *Turtle Wisdom: Coming Home to Yourself* was born.

Regardless of the harsh difficulties they brought to me, I honestly feel ultimately grateful for both my physical health imbalance and my childhood trauma because they inspired me to shift my emotional atmosphere to a place of appreciation, confidence, self-directed security, and peace.

The enduring inner resource which enabled me to cope with what was done to me as a child later motivated me to choose a profession in which I could help guide others through their struggles. It is an honor and a privilege to work with clients on both their current difficulties and in dealing with childhood and early adult trauma.

I have been asked to share some of my insights and strategies for embracing ourselves more fully. My experience with clients has shown me that this perspective can be helpful during times of crisis and trauma; yet I've also observed this approach being relevant for those who are simply trying to navigate the murky channels of daily life. Many of us have challenging experiences which are a catalyst for our expanded appreciation of self. But for those who have not, my wish is that by shifting your attention to it, you will be able to embrace more fully your sense of self without having to fall off the face of the earth first. Perhaps you can be saved from that journey. Because when all is said and done, if you are left with knowing and appreciating yourself, no matter what, then "that ain't bad!"

As I write this anniversary edition of the beloved *Turtle Wisdom: Coming Home to Yourself*, I've been witness to more recent examples of resilience and strength, one of the most obvious being our unprecedented global catastrophe. When the coronavirus pandemic hit, our world literally "shut down." People were confined in a way they hadn't ever been and new ways of being were forced to evolve. How we did business changed, how we related to our friends and family adjusted to the circumstance, and people found innovative methods to build community. In the process, there was so much loss ... many, many lives, old ways of living that no longer worked, and a sense of security that, for some, will never return.

> Yet, within each of us is a great well of strength and wisdom which can help us meet and master difficulties far beyond what we think we can handle. Even in the most difficult times, we can find what it is we need not only to survive, but to thrive. The key is to look within you; therein lies the knowledge, the understanding, and the wisdom of how to make it through. Meticulously excavate your golden nuggets, drawing forth the very best of you. That is your most valuable treasure! You are constantly reborn, living through your successes and your challenges by drawing forth more and more of that precious essence of your truest self. From that understanding, life becomes a great adventure, one to be embraced regardless of its twists and turns.
>
> It takes very little to make me happy these days. Me and my little mobile home—my "shell on my back"—are all I need. We will acquire the rest of what is desired in route on our next great adventure!
>
> One secures the gold of spirit when he finds himself.
>
> ~ Claude M. Bristol

Turtle Wisdom began with my clients wanting a "touchstone" between sessions. I wrote this book (in 2004) from that request thinking it would be read by perhaps a hundred or so people. Through a bold act of faith, I had it published, printing a thousand copies. I sold books directly to clients and friends and was able to display them in three local bookstores. Within a couple of weeks, I was attending a women's gathering facilitated by someone I didn't know. I was a guest brought to this circle by one of my close friends. As I sat perched on an ottoman I shared with my friend because every other seat in the room was taken, I watched as a woman (I'd never met) sitting across the circle from us, pulled *my* book from her purse. "I just read this wonderful book!" she said. "It is so encouraging. I'm carrying it around with me so I can read it whenever I need a boost in my day!" My friend beamed. "*This* is the author," she said as she pointed to me.

With no advertisement and no representation, in only five months I sold every one of those thousand copies. *Turtle Wisdom* had been shared like a warm hug, from friend to friend. And families often bought one copy, only to return to buy several so they could have one book for each family member. *Turtle Wisdom* was used as a reader in elementary schools, read aloud in community and social groups, and even used as the basis for an inspirational program in the county jail. The book started to gain interest internationally, too, as the timeless, universal message of *Turtle Wisdom* had a life of its own. And eighteen years later, still with very limited distribution, it continues to be a best-seller in some bookstores.

Now in 2023, *Turtle Wisdom: Coming Home to Yourself* has traveled around the globe, being published in 10 countries, world-wide in Chinese and Spanish. The turtle is a universal symbol of strength and resilience, held dear in many cultures. And recognizing that you are enough no matter where you are or what is going on, that your most precious resource is "you" is a message with universal truth. I hope it is one with meaning for you. May the little turtle continue to venture far and wide, including right into your very own heart.

> If I have lost every other friend on earth,
> I shall at least have one friend left,
> and that friend shall be down inside of me.
>
> ~ Abraham Lincoln

PART I

1

The Golden Opportunity is Within You

*The golden opportunity you are seeking is in yourself.
It is not in your environment, it is not in luck or chance,
or the help of others, it is in you alone.*

~ Orison Swett Marden

No matter what your life experience, your challenge, your turmoil, your joy, or your success, there is always one constant. One person who is always there, consistently present to all your encounters. When you choose to cultivate and draw strength and wisdom from within, you will never be deserted, never be fully defeated, but rather will discover layers upon layers of resilience within you. Like a turtle carting its shell, you carry what is truly essential within you.

When inspirational illustrator, author, and dear friend, Sue Lion, woke on a bone-dry day in December 2021, it seemed like any other winter day, this one with 100 mph winds. Sue always had many projects on her desk, so she got her cup of tea and dug in to her latest on the computer. Just after 11 am, her neighbor called with an urgent message, "Look out your window!" Flames were roaring at the fence line to the south. As Sue hastily packed up her computer and hard drives and ran to the car, she left with nothing else except the clothes on her back and her purse. She believed she would be returning to her cozy home of over 45 years—the firefighters were arriving. She had raised her children there and her grandchildren visited often. She did her design and artwork here, housed her fulfillment center, and hosted fellow authors and artists throughout the years. But hours later, after the firefighters had left to fight the voracious monster that eventually consumed almost 1,100 homes and burned 6,000 acres, chunks of fire burning in the ditch blew back into the neighborhood. Eight out of nine homes on the road lit up like torches and were fully destroyed, including Sue's. Every physical part of Sue's history burned up in an ominous black and orange cloud of fire—every piece of her personal belongings, her studio and original art, children's book collection, all the family photos, important papers, and books, including a newly released book recently delivered, were all reduced to ash. Sue's daughter's home was also destroyed a few miles away, while they were out of town to celebrate New Year's Eve. Sue hastily made her way through the back streets to save what little she could from their place in the midst of this unthinkable devastation.

Recovery took time. Another daughter and son-in-law opened their own home and gave her a place to heal. Friends and even strangers rallied. Local businesses provided aid. And Sue did a lot of inner work. It was not simple nor was it easy. But this resilient woman pulled herself through the thick and the thin of it, and now, over a year later, is well into the building of her new home. She is also rebuilding her inventory of reprinted artwork and reissued books, for what was thought to be gone is now being replaced with something new. Of course, many treasured possessions will never be replaced but were lost forever.

You may not have ever met Sue. But you have been touched by her in a way. She is my graphic designer and has illustrated many of my books, including creating this updated version of *Turtle Wisdom's* illustrations and graphic format. Sue continues to be an inspiration to those of us close to her as she begins anew in her seventies, rebuilding literally from the ground up.

Like Sue, you may have dear friends and family who support you, but when you lose a job, a marriage fragments, a loved one dies, or any event occurs that dramatically alters your life, no matter what, you still have yourself to turn to, to rely on. There is one person always available during the challenges and joys of every single day. Even in the most mundane moments when nothing particularly eventful is happening, who is there? You! By nurturing the evolution of the very best of that unique individual, you can develop a precious and rich commodity.

Many of us realize that there is an advantage to accepting and appreciating ourselves and striving to enhance that realization. When you nurture your mind with good thoughts and a belief that what you are doing is positive, even heroic, you create from that hero or heroine's state of mind. You are the hero or heroine of your own wisdom story.

Turtle Wisdom deepens that beneficial understanding. A turtle carries what she needs for shelter on her back. She chooses when to retreat into the protection of her shell and when to poke her head out; when to stand still and when to purposefully move forward.

People put their faith and trust in many outer things. They seek security, even validation in money, love from others, the kind of job they acquire, or some other aspect of outer-oriented security or prestige. Yet, these things are constantly changing and evolving. Nothing external can be counted on 100% to be there to support or nurture you. **There is only one thing that you can absolutely know and believe will be there for you no matter what. The one thing you can count on is YOU.**

Every day we are each presented with a fundamental option—to live from fear or from a sense of faith. Life is uncertain. Things change. People go away. Even the most unexpected may occur. How will you react to the shifting landscape? Cast your line upon the one constant. Why not develop the security you crave from others by finding it within yourself? Why not provide the nurturing you long for? Stop searching for it outside in the "hard, cruel world!" Instead of investing in one more self-help book or workshop, spend your precious time developing the most important relationship you'll ever have—your relationship with yourself.

Create the tenderness, support, and security you need from the inside out. If you weave an intricate web of safety based on who you are, what you stand for, and what you can contribute to this world, you will always have some semblance of security. If you base your thoughts, words, and actions on your own integrity, you will not be disappointed. And if you dwell in the presence of your Spiritual Source, in whatever way that has meaning for you, you will never be alone.

> Like the turtle, you carry your wisdom on your back. And as the wise old saying goes, "No matter where you go, there you are!" And no matter what happens, you will always have "you."

You are the one constant.

2

Sitting with Yourself

No matter where you go, there you are!

You have to begin where you are, but of course, the good news is you don't have to look far! Physically, at least, you know exactly where to find yourself. Go forward, there you are. Step back and there you are. Turn around and around and around and oops! There you are again. Sometimes life experiences are kind of like that—move this way and that, almost in an attempt to escape yourself and yet at every turn, there you are staring yourself in the face.

Stop. Take a good look. Assess how you approach life. How comfortable are you in your own skin? Now that might sound like a crazy question, but entertain it honestly:

- Have you settled into the physical container of your body? Do you like being in there?
- Do you feel at home there?
- Is it good to wake up to yourself in the morning? Do you have a sense of excitement for what the day may bring?
- Do you enjoy your own company? Is it okay to be alone?

Make an agreement to appreciate the aspects you like about yourself and to improve the parts you'd like to change. Develop your confident and secure inner core being, the essential part of you that truly expresses your unique qualities and giftedness. Those are the pieces that make you—well, you! Draw that precious essence forth and ground it into your life expression.

- Recognize the beautiful, complex, and unique creation you are. Remember you are unveiling a masterpiece through the life you live.
- Notice how you show up in your daily life.
- How do you impact those around you?
- What contributions do you make to the greater expression of life? Observe your impact on the world (even the smallest ones).
- What footprints do you leave upon the earth? What we say and do reverberates long after the moment they are birthed ... and remain long after we are physically gone.

Your life is not about the roles you play, the careers you've pursued, or the money and possessions you acquire. And the world-wide Covid epidemic taught us that it isn't even just about our health status. Much can be gained or lost in any given moment. Life, at its core, is about how you develop as a human being; it's about your soul evolution. Are you creating more satisfaction within you, more joy, more love? Feel into your life as fully as possible and make conscious choices about how you live that life. Have gratitude for life's opportunity.

Be mindfully present so you can truly meet yourself with all the time and attention you would invest in something or someone precious. You are a diamond. You may be polished or still in the rough, either way you are precious beyond measure. Deepen your understanding of who you are and who you are becoming. Delight in the process and celebrate the beauty of your unique sparkle. You are a brilliant gem!

Physical Assessment

Let's begin by focusing on the physical. How often do you take a physical assessment? I am not asking about the times you look in the mirror and notice that you need to visit the hairdresser, or perhaps notice that you've acquired a new wrinkle. Neither is it when you dress and check out your wardrobe in the reflection.

- Do you notice how your body feels?
- Are there physical parts that you can sense and others that you do not?
- Are there places where you feel harmoniously interconnected?
- Are there others where one part tugs on another creating tension or stress?
- Does your vital life force flow easily and fully through your entire physical form?

Try this simple focal process: Take time to sit in a quiet place and notice your body. You can start at the top of your head and move slowly downward taking inventory as you move with your awareness.

- Where is there tightness, tension, or pain?
- What feels stuck?
- Or numb?
- Just observe, without judgement, and you may learn something important to your physical wellbeing.

You cannot treat something unless you are aware of it. In our busy society, there have been cases of people who developed cancerous growths or other physical imbalances, but did not seek treatment, because they were so detached from their physical bodies that they did not feel the warning symptoms. Aside from that, sometimes simply acknowledging how a certain part of your body feels can be enough to help it to feel better. By just noticing a numb part, you can draw vital energy to that area. By noticing an imbalance, you may alter your diet or exercise or minimize physical stress; thereby restoring your body's natural balance. There may be parts of you crying for attention. Take the time to listen.

Inner Exploration
a contemplation piece

Now, let's move our focus inside of you. Read the following contemplation and then close your eyes and meditate on it.

Take a deep breath. Relax. Center on yourself as you draw your attention inward. Allow any external distractions to subside as they lose the ability to pull you out of or away from your intended focus. Any disturbance simply melts away as you journey fully and completely inside yourself ....

Imagine a road going off into the distant horizon. See the path ahead winding this way and that. Notice if there are subtle colors or vibrant hues along the path. Is the area you see lush and alive with growth? Are there wildflowers nearby? Or is it dry, barren brown? Just observe what comes to mind. If a picture does not appear, just notice what you feel or what you think of in the next few moments ....

Off in the distance, you see movement along the path. You watch with anticipation, as you know, instinctively, that what is approaching is of great importance. You know it in your gut. You know it in your bones. Your anticipation builds as the rustling grows closer. What is coming toward you?

The object of fascination comes closer and closer. Closer and closer ... closer and closer. And finally, you catch a glimmer. There is a familiarity there, but you cannot quite place it. Something seems known, and yet at the same time, strange and new.

The picture grows clearer now, and with awe and wonderment, you gaze upon the most amazing thing.

It is you! You have met yourself along the path.
You have encountered yourself coming and going
and there you are—together.
The two of you.
You and "you."

And what do you see? Notice her carefully. Observe every detail with fascination.

And what do you feel? Observe what you sense about this person. Is she happy or sad? Content or restless? Tired or vibrant? Do you *like* her? You may feel connected to her immediately, or it may take some time to get to know her.

As you view this traveler on the road, are you able to engage her in conversation, laughter, and friendship? Can you sit your bodies down and have tea? Notice if you are repulsed by this image of your self, somehow pushing her away, shutting her out. Or are you simply disinterested? Be honest with this first impression. It is important beyond measure.

Knowing yourself affects every journey, every road you take. Your awareness moves and vibrates in the very breath of life which sustains you. It is at the root of all you do. Until we have met ourselves and taken stock, how can we know how we relate, deep down, to the person we are? And if we do not know how we relate, how can we develop that important relationship? We need to tend it like a sacred garden, giving it nourishment and nurturing, so that it may blossom into something greater and greater. Evolution is the very nature of life. Our life longs to expand and express further, to become more, to experience more. There is an innate divine urge within you that is pushing to create through you. Can you feel it? Be open to knowing its presence ... and clear the way so it might come into its rightful form.

So, sit with this vision of your meeting on the path. Journal about it. Contemplate it over the coming days. It is from this point that we begin and from this initial relationship that we build.

Earth School: What Classes are You Taking?

Our time here on earth is one of higher learning. Like school, there are lessons that are required and as such, we have no choice but to encounter those circumstances and embrace the curriculum. Some people turn their entire attention to what is "required" of them.

- What about those times when you might determine the direction of your pursuits?
- Do you poke around in the wilderness of the unknown, the never-before-explored?
- Do you try on new hats as variations of being yourself? Do you express new facets of your personality?

- Do you allow yourself to change directions and embark on a new path of discovery?
- Are you embracing opportunities as points of choice? Are you actively exploring them?

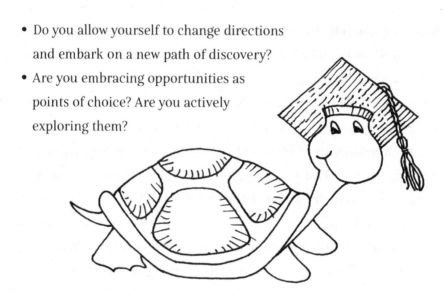

What is your heart's desire? Your soul's craving?
You owe it to yourself to explore and pursue these longings.

You owe it to those you love to do so, too. Some of us live our lives meeting other people's needs, fulfilling obligations, doing what we think we "should" do. It can be exhausting. There is no time or energy left over to explore our own personal interests. Our life's schedule is chock full of requirements, leaving no room for the enjoyment of our electives! If this sounds like you, pause for a minute and consider: If you continually sacrifice for others and do not pursue your heart's passion, you may become hopelessly depleted, even dried up, giving from a sense of obligation rather than desire. And in that manner, even the helpful and good actions you do will suffer.

> **What is your heart's desire? Your soul's craving?**
> **You owe it to yourself to explore and pursue these longings.**
> - What do you hope for?
> - What direction do you want to take?
> - What experiences do you wish to have?
> - What brings you joy?
> - Do you have an inner desire pushing to be acknowledged?
> - Integrate these personal pursuits into your life, balancing them with your obligations. When you are fulfilled, your happiness or contentment is overflowing; you have much more to offer. As you replenish your vitality by doing the things you love, simply because you love to do them, your natural joy impacts those around you.

Recognize yourself as the appropriate, intended focus of your lifetime and the world will open with opportunity. You can make time for that French class or save for your dream cruise.

I've discovered something remarkable through a lifetime of working with women. **Often, we can engage in a desired activity for as little as fifteen minutes a day with tangible benefits.** I've challenged those with even the most demanding schedules to carve out little pockets of time to immerse themselves in what they desire and to note how this makes them feel. The CEO of a company found enhanced productivity the result of reading a book of her choice for just fifteen minutes a day. With stacks of reports screaming for attention on her desk, this simple pleasure was one she had previously denied herself. Giving into that sweet desire reaped unexpected results. A young mother longed to create a vision board, but busy days with her little ones didn't afford the luxury of much quiet time for herself. After exploring possibilities, she decided to engage them and even at five and seven-years-old, she found that her children loved the activity! They each had their own stack of magazines and after she explained that they could rip out pictures about what they liked—things they wanted to bring into their lives—she was astounded at the deep thought and somewhat "grown up" concepts they demonstrated. Instead of pictures of toys, like a bike or a train set, her children had pictures of families around a barbecue or in the yard playing with the family dog. They were drawn to pictures with feelings that they saw as desirable: togetherness and fun, family time. This mom got even more from her kids' vision boards than she did from her own! And those vision boards remain dated and framed, displayed prominently in their home to this day, decades after their joyful afternoon creating them together.

You are your life's creation. Invest the time, energy, and financial resources to create a masterpiece.

Goals and Intentions: Your Approach to Life

Goals are ideas for what you want to experience or achieve and strategies for obtaining your desire. They are future oriented. You organize your time and energy to work toward goals. Goals create a structure from which to live your life. Achievement of one goal often leads to setting subsequent goals.

Intentions are driven by your most significant values and your choice of how to live from those values. Intentions are focused more on your way of being in the world. They are seasoned with your attitudes and beliefs. Whether or not you consciously identify them, you live from your intentions every day, as they shape how you relate to each and every moment that presents itself.

When living from your own authenticity, whatever you experience can be an integral part of your life, a meaningful exploration and an opportunity to express who you are in a contributing manner. Instead of your eye being focused on some predestined vision of what you want to achieve, your most important life gauge becomes being true to yourself.

Being aware of your intentions can help you to better achieve your goals, since this focus can enhance your ability to gracefully move with all the changes in life. In times of stress or turmoil, intentions can help you to stay focused on what is truly important to you, independent of any particular outcome. Intentions create an inner peace that is not affected by the turmoil of the outer world.

Consider these brief examples:

GOAL: To find a job that I like and be paid well.

🐢 INTENTION: To share my unique gifts at every opportunity and develop into the best that I can be. To know my contributions are valuable and to appreciate the many ways I can give. I accept the understanding that I deserve to be rightfully compensated for my contributions.

GOAL: To have a mate

🐢 INTENTION: To be a loving expression in all I do with all I meet. To open to a greater expression of love in my life.

GOAL: For my children's issues to be resolved

🐢 INTENTION: To be a calming, positive resource to my children without visualizing or manipulating any specific outcome to the issues they now face. I trust in their ability to navigate their own matters and simply support them by knowing they are capable.

> Louise came to me because she was distraught over not having spoken to her adult daughter for several years. She greatly missed not only her daughter but her grandchildren and although she sent cards and gifts, she had no idea if the children even received them. She had a very specific agenda about how she wanted things to be. In working together, I helped Louise step aside from her diligence of trying to force anything from happening in the manner she desired, and instead, identified Louise's authentic desire to share a harmonious, mutually beneficial relationship with her daughter and her family. We focused time and energy on her clear intention of wanting to be a part of her daughter's

family. A welcomed change occurred remarkably fast! Just a few short days later, Louise's daughter reached out through an unsolicited phone call. The conversation was relaxed and easy-going. "It seemed so natural!" Louise reported. The two women made plans to get together the following week and to spend a part of a day with the entire family over the holidays. By shifting her own limiting perspective, Louise experienced what felt like miraculous results. And the positive change has continued. Louise feels "very blessed to watch the grandkids grow up." Once she let go of pushing her own agenda, an energetic shift occurred, altering the outer picture of circumstance as everything seemed to click right into place. Isn't it remarkable how that happens?

Explore your own list of goals and intentions. You can be much more detailed with your specifications. For activities to support you in this process, refer to the *Turtle Wisdom Playbook: A Motivational Coloring Adventure!*

What if?

What if you recognized yourself as your biggest asset? You can always make more money, get a new home, even rebuild, or change relationships. The one person that you can never escape is yourself. You are there at every turn, at every life challenge and every life joy. You are the person you need to deal with day in and day out—your highs, your lows, and all of the in-betweens. You are the one constant.

So, what if you truly valued this person whose skin you live in, whose steps are your own and whose path is your way? What if you treated yourself as if you were your greatest treasure? What if you understood that you are a precious, unique gift to this world? What if you praised your successes and felt the fullness of those successes? What if you tenderly supported yourself through your challenges with the patience you might show a small child? What if you awoke each day with a song of gratitude for this earthly existence and with anticipation for what the day might bring? What would your life be like then?

3
No One Else Can Do It!

> Destiny is not a matter of chance, it is a matter of choice;
> it is not a thing to be waited for, it is a thing to be achieved.
>
> *~ William Jennings Bryan*

> Everyone is self-made. Only the successful people admit it.
>
> *~ Unknown*

Whether or not you decide to fully live your life, you are the only one who can do it. No one else can do it for you. Yet some among us are like walking zombies, trudging from one thing to another, not making choices or living with intent. Coming from that perspective, one is not feeling the fullness of what they experience, the richness of their personal connections, nor the true joy of their accomplishments. There is an ever-pervading numbness, denying them the fullest intensity of their life experience.

Have you ever encountered someone who has had a near death experience? Perhaps you, yourself, have had one? After having such a close call, a person often has a keen sense of appreciation, savoring moments that the rest of us let slip by unnoticed for their beauty. It is my hope that more of us may come to know the precious and bountiful gift of life in a way that elevates our collective consciousness and enables us to do greater things in the time given to us.

Let's begin by imagining that we are gathered in a supportive circle, sitting on the ground together, and sensing an appreciation for Mother Earth beneath us. Our inherent connection with the natural world provides a sound universal practice to strengthen our earthly connection. Although we are spiritual beings, we are here on the physical plane for a reason and to be fully connected with the Earth supports us in that mission. We build an important foundation which energetically supports everything we do. And as earth guardians, we also live in a manner which respects and honors our planet—each and every respectful action toward her matters, all our little actions add up. Be conscious of what you do and walk gently upon the earth.

Mud Pies

Did you play in the dirt as a child? Did you walk bare foot in the grass or play in muddy puddles after it rained? Let's go back to the dirt.

Do you take time every day to connect with the earth beneath your feet? I know that may sound ridiculous, but I am quite serious. Some people hit the ground running and don't stop until they lay their heads back down at night. It is a wonder that they are tethered to world at all—thank goodness for gravity! I want to suggest a simple practice, which can enhance your connection and provide the stability of a much stronger base. This activity is best done outside, while firmly standing on the ground. In inclement weather or other situations when being outdoors is not possible, you can use this technique indoors and simply imagine the earth beneath your feet.

Stand with your feet firmly planted on the earth beneath you. It's best to stand with your feet comfortably spaced at about a hips width apart providing a strong base for your pelvis and legs. Just notice how it feels to be conscious of the land holding you up, supporting you ... Open yourself to any sensations in your feet, your legs, and on up through the body. Many people feel a vibration, a tingling energy, or simply a warmth radiating up and through their physical form. When you open to what sensations may be there, you might be surprised at how much you do feel when you take the time to tap in and listen. Just let go of any preconceived expectations and notice what is there for you.

Now imagine tiny roots growing from your feet into the earth and then larger roots and finally a very prominent taproot going deep, deep within the earth, holding you safely and securely on this earthly plane ... grounding you firmly in our world. If you do not actually feel it, then imagine it.

Now notice what you sense coming from the earth, and what you sense in your body, and how your sensations may have changed during this focused process. How is it to feel rooted? Be aware of the energetic nourishment you receive through your roots; it's there even when you are unaware of it.

Recognize that you are connected—rooted—to the earth and through those roots you receive support in your daily endeavors. Like the trees, you are fed with nourishment. Focusing on this natural energetic flow and being consciously aware of its occurrence can enhance its effectiveness and assist you in approaching your day from a more grounded, steady stance.

Try this technique for a week and observe how your days unfold.

> My friend, Emilia, has an unusual past. In October 2002, she was part of a radical group of protesters who took to the redwoods in California in an effort to keep them from being cut down. She actually climbed up in a tree ... and did not come down for nine months. Food and water were trucked in and hoisted up to the small platform she called home. Her waste was carted out in the same manner.
>
> Emilia speaks about how fast things manifest "in the trees." She says that she became vigilant about her thoughts because even the simplest one seemed to come to pass very quickly. "I haven't had a flan in a while. I can almost taste it!" and that afternoon, a piece came up in her delivery bucket. She also received a spool of climbing rope and a headlamp for much-needed light, in the same manner, without verbally requesting them.
>
> Her primitive experience had profound repercussions too. This woman, a caretaker of the earth in so many ways— she's a landscaper, a gardener, a farmer, and a horsewoman— speaks about the tree holding her, about how she came to know the language of that tree and could understand the warning when inclement weather was coming, and about

how in the beginning she used her climbing ropes, but after
a short time knew the path, whether it was in visible daylight
or the darkness of the night, and how she could make her
way to the tippy top of that two-hundred-twenty-five-foot
redwood, to sit and gaze into the horizon.

I never sat in a tree for any length of time. In fact, even as a child,
I wasn't drawn to it. As a city kid I was much more likely to be found
on a rooftop than in a tree. Yet, when I listen to Emilia's stories, there is
a place deep within me that stirs. A place in which I know and treasure
that soul connection with the trees. Emilia helps me to remember.

> Be like a tree in pursuit of your cause.
> stand firm, grip hard, thrust upward,
> bend to the winds of heaven,
> and learn tranquility.
>
> *Dedication to*
> *Richard St. Barbe Baker*
> *Father of the Trees*

Live in a manner which acknowledges, respects, and honors the
Earth that holds you up and supports you every day in so many ways.
Walk gently upon the Mother beneath you.

> I entrust myself to the earth,
> Earth entrusts herself to me.
>
> *~ Thich Nhat Hahn*

You get You

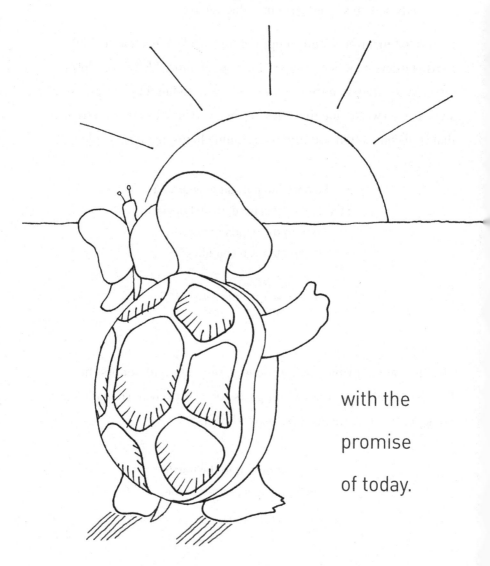

with the

promise

of today.

4

How Does Your Garden Grow? Cultivating a Truer You

A garden requires patient labor and attention. Plants do not grow merely to satisfy ambitions or to fulfill good intentions. They thrive because someone expended effort on them.

~ Liberty Hyde Bailey

"Mary, Mary quite contrary how does your garden grow?" goes the well-known nursery rhyme. You've most likely heard it as a child. The idea of a garden doesn't have to be just about describing a physical plot of land in your backyard. When you are "coming home to yourself," the idea of a **personal (inner) garden** is helpful to consider how the natural process of creation takes place ... and how you might optimize your harvest with what you need and want.

Gardens are nurtured: from preparing the soil, to planting the seeds, fertilizing and watering the new sprouts, removing smothering weeds, and harvesting when your babies are at their best. Gardens are purposefully cared for, some more than others, surely, but even the

most neglected garden holds a marked memory of care and attention. At one time, it was loved.

When it comes to a garden, you get what you plant. You can't look at the solid ground and scream, "I want carrots!" and expect anything to happen. You can't fall to your knees and cry hysterically, begging, "Please, oh please, give me carrots." You can't even implore, "If you loved me, you'd bring me carrots. Where are my carrots?"

If YOU want carrots, you *must* PLANT carrots!

And if you've always planted something else—let's say zucchini, yellow squash, or peas—your understanding of how to plant, where to plant, when to plant, and how to harvest in regards to these crops may be deeply understood. Their blueprint may literally be ingrained in the very essence of the soil. The same is true for our old, established personality patterns which are remarkably familiar, even second nature. Your old ways may be suitable for what you've always "planted" through your actions in life, but these old patterns may not be optimal for inspiring a new or different "crop." If you decide to plant something different, conscious thought and careful preparation will ensure you can make the shift in an efficient and effective manner. You amend the soil.

Choice is a powerful part of our process: when we focus on what we actually want to grow, we often receive precious intuitive insights as to how to help facilitate change. When we know what we need, it's easier to amend the soil to provide the necessary nutrients; to fine-tune our attitudes and behaviors to optimize our intended growth.

Life can change if you develop new patterns of being or apply yourself in new ways. But to do so you may need to make outer shifts in your environment or personality changes within you. You might have to let go of attitudes, beliefs, and behaviors that no longer serve you and form new pathways to follow.

In addition, if you want to plant tomatoes, you most likely will acquire a strong stick to support the vine. If you want to plant a delicate flower or a rare breed, you might consult a master gardener. In this same way, you may want to draw in additional support—a mentor or a guide—as you learn to grow something different and new. Each one of us is a rare breed, having unique needs and desires for our personal healing, development, and growth. Look around you and reach out to those who can support the changes you wish to make; those who can help you be cared for and nurtured as you grow ... and those who can hold the vision for you of what's possible, until you can hold it for yourself. Fashion your "inner life garden" so it serves you best.

Right now, regardless of what time of the year or what season it is; regardless of what the weather of your external or internal environment; regardless of any presence or lack of a particular factor; right now, is a wonderfully fertile time to prepare your inner soil for new growth and to consider exactly what kind of **"seeds of intention"** you want to plant. You have all the impetus you need to infuse your day with extra energy to tackle your own personal development project!

> Watching gardeners label their plants, I vow with all beings to practice the old horticulture and let the plants identify me.
>
> ~ Robert Aitken

Our lives are beautiful landscapes, rich with variations of color and texture. How we plant, nurture, and grow our gardens is quite individual. Some plots are neglected, badly in need of fertilizer and water; they are overrun with weeds, scraggly pitiful plants, and useless debris. Others are glorious, radiating a colorful vibrant beauty because they have been tended carefully with loving attention. Some gardens are delicate with rare specimens, while others are rugged, withstanding very harsh conditions. How do you cultivate your life? **Take a walk in your "garden" and notice what you see.**

How does your garden grow? Take an assessment.
- Where are you right now? What is happening? What are you cultivating?
- What do you see growing? Are you happy with what you are growing?
- Is it what you wish to harvest? Or is it lacking in some way?
- Make a conscious choice to be more mindful of what you attract toward you.
- Make a conscious choice to be more mindful about what you put out from you.
- And, of course, you can choose to fine-tune your inner garden, so you might reap an even richer harvest, by expressing more and more of who you are authentically.
- Reveal your truest self (she's beautiful, you know).

> Always be on the lookout
> for the presence of wonder.
>
> ~ E. B. White

Be open to what you see in your garden. Honestly assess yourself and your life. Notice the variations of your personality, the nuances of who you are. Determine what is in full bloom and what is still growing. Be aware of the seeds that could be tended carefully so they may blossom. Be open to elements that may be missing and could be transplanted into your garden. Cultivate your potential so you may better express your authentic self. Accept where you are—with the vision of where you might grow to be. Just as you would appreciate a meandering walk in a fine garden, be open to the discovery of the richness of who you are and what is your life's landscape. Know that each element with its unique variation is an integral part of the whole. Appreciate your own bountiful garden as it is right now ... as well as envisioning the potential of what
it might be.

> Recognize and accept
> the beauty of who you are.
>
> ~ Turtle Wisdom

You are a part of the Divine Plan. It is your birthright to create through your unique expression in and through your unique experiences. You do not need to do anything to prove your worthiness. You do not need to earn the right to receive this creative spark, this influx of life force energy. It is your birthright to receive creative energy and to bring forth your creations just for you.

By acknowledging this natural gift, every moment becomes precious, every experience contributes to the collective as nothing is insignificant. Who you are matters and how you live your life matters, too. Your little "neck of the woods" (your life's scope) and what happens there impacts the whole even if others aren't directly a part of those happenings. Energy moves outward, rippling in greater and greater rings of impact that may not be seen by the naked eye, but are felt way beyond their reach. Make a conscious choice to be more mindful about what you put into the world. Your actions plant seeds of possibility for the future; they are one powerful way to tend the soul of our world.

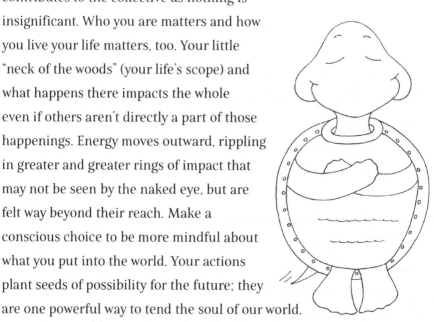

Accepting your honored place in the grand circle of life and realizing the value in your own backyard enhances your appreciation of the everyday, the mundane. Even going to the grocery store can become an important adventure! You never know who you might meet or what you might see. It's all a significant step on the path of life.

> When you begin to know rather
> than doubt your talent,
> you will discover the necessary physical abilities
> to carry out your purpose.
>
> ~ *Wayne Dyer*

You *belong here!* It was no mistake that you were born. There is something so precious and unique about you. No one else is exactly like you. You have the ability to bring a contribution to this world that no one else can make; without you that piece would be lost. Accept your own importance and consider your place in the larger ecosystem of *all of life*.

- What part do you play? In what roles do you serve?
- How do you impact those around you?
- What actions reach beyond?
- And in what ways is there still untapped potential within you? What is the greater plan?

> Each time you do these contemplations come back to center and ask, "What are my wildest dreams and my sweetest happiness?" Now, how can I create *that* in my life!

I offer a yearly program at the dawn of each new year, called "Power Boost." We focus on personal and group processes that tap our understanding and potential for that year. One of the simplest, yet often profound considerations is what word or phrase you want to use as a focal mantra for that year. This year mine was, "Bigger is not necessarily better." During a year (2023) when I have several writing projects on my desk, including this anniversary rewrite, I chose to pull myself in and let go of commitments and tasks not in alignment with the productivity necessary to accomplish what was before me. Sometimes we strive to do everything without considering how it fits into our overall plan. This simple mantra helps me steer the course for heightened awareness and practical accomplishment.

In a garden, the most beautiful blossom or the largest tree does not necessarily serve the greatest purpose. All parts matter. One gorgeous, showy flower may attract many pollinators, helping the garden with her obvious beauty. Another nondescript little green shoot may not immediately catch your eye but could hold the promise of a grand fruit tree, spending this season pushing her new roots down into the earth, so that she may find her footing to grow tall and wide, providing shade and bearing sweet fruit. If we can observe our own endeavors as we might observe this garden, we can appreciate all the aspects of our lives, recognizing them as the building blocks or necessary steps moving us forward into the evolution of life.

> I am "who I am" every step of the way, authentically me—
> and I'm discovering and rediscovering who I am
> each day through my experiences ...
> I accept all parts of me,
> even the ones that don't look pretty.
> Each piece of me
> serves a purpose
> even when I can't see it.
> Each part contributes to the whole of who I am.
>
> ~ *Turtle Wisdom*

Be aware of what's beyond the surface. Open to sensing and reading the "vibes" in the room. Notice how what you think, say, and do affects others and how their words and actions impact you.

What is seasoning your interactions? Is something happening on another level? Observe those times when the content of what someone is saying does not fully match what you feel he or she means. His emotions may not be congruent with his words, or he may be thinking one thing and saying something else. There are many possibilities to what is truly happening when the communication pieces are not quite fitting together. And of course, observe your own style of sharing, too.

We often limit our awareness of what is available in the world by seeing through the filters of our own limited surface vision. Opening to the possibility of what might be transpiring multi-dimensionally, both at the surface and in the depths below, can greatly expand our vision. Strive to optimize your awareness of what is happening on *all levels of interaction*. When you notice the subtle influences around you, you will discover an energetic playground to explore! Delight in the interplay of your particular and unique vibration as it interfaces with others and be open to sensing energetic nuances. By considering these energetic patterns, you can observe how they affect you and your experiences. By becoming aware of this subtle dance, you can make more deliberate choices about how to meet and manage situations.

When you are more conscious about observing and working directly with this energy, you will enhance your interpersonal communication and interpersonal connections.

Another fascinating measurement is to **observe when you are sharing from your head, when from your heart, and when from a combination of the two.** Many of us lead from a good, strong intellect and although this may be effective to draw on the capable mind, it is often more potent to season that content with our heart's perceptive knowing. As we exchange ideas, we aim to have our point of view seen or our message received with the clarity with which we intended it. The fuller this message is, the more apt it is to be received with its rightful intention. Drawing from the head and the heart with a balance appropriate to the situation, assures its success in growing the conversation as well as the relationship with those you're conversing with. I've seen "bosses" interacting with friends and family members with the same authority and direct language as they use when giving a command to a subordinate. This does not often go well!

> When I've been the recipient of this kind of language, my reaction is, "I don't work for you!" In relating to one such head honcho, my consistent pointing out of the tone or wording of his request resulted not only in a change of how he communicated with me, but also an observable difference in how he interacted with his employees. And of course, this has circled back around with improvements in how family, friends, and employees communicate with him. Tempering the clear, direct messaging of the head with the understanding of how people want to be spoken to and doing so with kindness from the heart has given his words new growth, as they've blossomed into a fruitful fullness.

No matter what the unrest,
there is an underlying calm.
No matter what the emotional trauma,
there is an inner peace.
No matter what the apparent discord,
there is a basic harmony.
No matter what the physical imbalance,
there is perfect, complete healing.
No matter how dark it might seem,
there is ever-present, ever-nurturing Light.
Look within to your own deeply rooted understanding
of peace, harmony, and total well-being.
Allow the fertile seed to burst forth
into creative life expression,
blooming with multi-colored vibrant beauty
for all to see!

~ Donna DeNomme, 1992

So, let's take a closer look at the various aspects of what helps your garden grow as you cultivate a truer you.

Design Your Own Landscape

You can allow your garden to grow wild and free or choose to meticulously sculpt it into elaborate configurations or anything in between. There is no one "right" way. Design your life as you choose. Create a garden which is your very own.

Tilling the Soil—Preparation

> Seek goodness everywhere,
> and where it is found,
> bring it out of its hiding place
> and let it be free and unashamed.
>
> ~ William Saroyan

We began with a powerful realization that life itself craves individualized expression through you and that it is unfolding within the context of your personal experience. There is an order and a meaning to all that occurs. Just as the plant's withering in the fall is as much a part of the cycle of life as the spring's sprout; so too, all pieces of your life are natural contributions—the challenges and the successes, the turmoil as well as the joy, the active growth and the resting places. Look beyond the surface to the deeper meaning of where you are at any given moment. Open to see and appreciate the contribution it serves.

What's Under the Surface: In-Sight

Nature creates in mysterious and magnificent ways. There is a remarkable force we observe in the vast and varied expression of the natural world. You have an innate connection with the same essential source of life. There is great insight and wisdom within this source and there is innate knowledge and wisdom within you, too. You have access to this guidance and instinctively know how to live and grow from this inner connection. Allow that strong, ever-present impulse to thrive; allow it the space to sprout and grow.

Cultivate an unshakable trust in your in-sights, as you develop an openness to the understanding, inner support, and intuitive guidance that comes from them. One way to do this is through free style or stream of consciousness writing, especially in the morning. Others find meditative pauses throughout their day helpful in developing this important inner (and higher) connection. You might take a look at *As You Feel, So You Heal: A Write of Passage*, a beautifully illustrated, full-color, hard cover keepsake book if you'd like to develop more in this area of accessing your inner realm. It is a treasure trove of practical practices.

> You can prepare
> the fertile soil of your
> creative life expression
> by learning to trust
> your inner knowing.
>
> *~ Turtle Wisdom*

You can develop your ability to access the knowledge and wisdom available to you—through you. Notice and acknowledge those precious moments when you absolutely know what's right and true because your strong inner sense is so assured ... and stretch to sense its presence when it isn't so obvious. Ask yourself probing questions and listen for the answers that well up and come from within. Some people think this intuitive knowing is a gift saved for a certain few, but it can be developed by your attention to it; your receptivity and attentive listening are the nourishment that helps this finicky "plant" grow!

> When you recognize and utilize the intuitive realm, it will open your personal scope. You will be inspired in new directions, able to take risks and experiment in unfamiliar ways for the sheer curiosity of discovering what might be.

I'm one who appreciates stability and can happily live with consistency. I don't necessarily get bored with repetition of daily patterns. Yet I marvel at the experiences that have come in like a bolt of lightning, super-fast and bright, and have shifted my life in some dramatic way. One time, years ago, I was asked kind-of-last-minute to fly to Mexico and lead meditations on the beach. Now, I must tell you that, at the time, I did not fly. I just didn't. I was quite satisfied to focus on what was around me—I had plenty to do—and my field of vision was kind of narrow in that way. But something within me beckoned to accept that invitation, so I joined a group of women on a stunningly gorgeous white sandy beach bordering the turquoise crystal-clear waters in Isla Mujeres, Mexico, for a week-long retreat. Paradise! This one retreat led to me leading spiritual retreats to the Yucatan five times a year for six years! Unexpected, surely. Delightful—definitely. And my shift was a benefit to the greater whole, as well, as groups of sixteen to eighteen people found comfort, healing, and expansive growth during those excursions. Sometimes in stretching to bring forth a new balance within us, we also help to rebalance that greater whole of a larger community beyond ourselves.

> Helpful habits can be good and I'm not suggesting you strive to change them, but at times your stability may become stagnant. Life itself might spontaneously modify your pattern by stretching toward a new way of being that moves your personal evolution forward. Life is always evolving in those greater circles of expression. Open your horizon and delight in the potential for the self-discovery of what might be pushing to express. When you value your intuitive self, and temper it with your heart's wisdom, you can carefully remove the debris of self-doubt and unworthiness, as you till the soil for a hearty new crop.

Planting—Conscious Choice

Within you are *many, many seeds of potential*, which are the uniqueness of who you are. Conscious choice enables you to choose what to create in your experience by the selection of what you choose to "plant." Conscious living enables you to create in alignment with who you truly are at the core of your being. Sometimes your choices are obvious ones and ones that make total sense. At other times, your choices may not necessarily make the most logical sense but are driven from within you, from that place of your deep inner knowing and then your actions back up or reinforce those deliberate choices. You act as if what you desire to be or do *already* is your reality. And those trusting actions set up a force field which attracts that very thing into your being.

"Aerodynamically the bumble bee shouldn't be able to fly,
but the bumble bee doesn't know it
so it goes on flying anyway."

~ Mary Kay Ash

Know that what you think, say, and do has an impact on your life experience. You must act in alignment with what you are wanting to grow in your garden. If you focus on failure, you will never cultivate success; isolation will not cultivate love; erratic spending is not a viable seed of abundant prosperity.

> Conscious living
> allows you to create your life
> in alignment with who you truly
> are at the core of your being.
>
> ~ Turtle Wisdom

Say what you mean and mean what you say. Take full responsibility for your thoughts, words, and actions. Observe yourself and check for alignment with what you really desire. Be cautious when you are in a defensive reaction and instead, shift to show up purposefully in alignment with your personal intentions. And if you put something out there which, upon reflection, is *not really* what you wanted to place into the vibrational sphere, then you can follow it up with steps to alter, or even to neutralize its impact. Know, also, that you possess the ability to neutralize the impact of what others say and do pertaining to you. Refer to Difficult Days (chapter 8, page 142) for more on these topics.

We are what we think.
All that we are arises with our thoughts.
Speak and act with a pure mind and happiness will follow.
The wind cannot overturn the mountain,
like temptation cannot touch those
who are awake, strong, and humble. Fill yourself with desire.
See the false, as false, the true as true.
Look into your heart, and follow your nature.
Know these truths and you will find peace.

~ Buddha

When it comes to conscious choice, recognize that within you is the preciousness of the seed, which is germinating into the sprout that can be nurtured into the hearty plant, blossoming into all its beauty. Let go of the criticisms that stifle the growth of your potential. Turn your understanding and acceptance to the newness, which is within, and give it the time and the space to mature.

Putting Up the Scarecrow –

Creating Your Own Safety

We've been exploring who you are and what you do as the "crop" you are growing. Observe if you allow others to trample on that creation in a way that is destructive. Are people infringing on your personal space or the fruits of your time and energy? Do not allow the "crows" to eat your growing crop! You must protect yourself, so you can reap your precious harvest.

- Do you feel safe? Or does the world seem threatening to you?
- Are you able to move with the rhythms of life, making adjustments when necessary?
- Do you have a healthy autonomy or do people encroach upon your personal boundaries in a way which irritates you?
- Do you even have personal boundaries?
  "Personal boundaries. Huh? What is that?!?"
  (Ah, now that's a problem).

> What is a personal boundary? Healthy boundaries are not about building a fortress around you, complete with a moat filled with alligators to nip at any intruders to the castle. It is about creating safety so you can have dominion over yourself and can be free to explore the greater world, enjoying the grand adventure of life.

One important personal boundary is maintaining agency over your own physical form, your body. It is about being physically safe. It is having what the body needs such as food, exercise, and rest. It is not allowing or being subject to anyone breaching those boundaries in a way that infringes on your physical space. In its extreme forms, this would be violence or physical abuse; more subtle forms may be more difficult to recognize. Ask yourself: do I have control over my own body? Or does someone else mandate what it receives and how it's treated?

Another important personal boundary is having the mental space for your own thoughts without them being controlled by another. Other people provide ideas and information, which you consider in the realm of your intellect, but you have ultimate dominion over your thoughts. You are free to be who you are, and you can rest assured that you exist because you are the one doing the thinking. "I think, therefore I am." (Descartes, 1637).

Another important personal boundary is having the healthy emotional separation to be free to experience your emotions in a way which allows you to meet them, learn from, and deal with them in appropriate ways. You cultivate an emotional intelligence based on your own emotional temperament and the experiences that help your emotions evolve. You are free to feel.

Consider methods to physically, mentally, emotionally, and energetically protect yourself. Explore what you need to do to be more protected, to feel safer in each of these areas. Fine-tune and develop security that is constant and dependable. Grow your internal assurance, rather than counting on an external source that may change or disappear over time. Then, regardless of the outer realities, you can stand on that secure ground within yourself, based on your own capable ability to move within the changes of what life brings.

There are many practices that can be done to protect yourself. What is most important is to recognize that **you are ultimately responsible**

for creating your own safety. And for you to learn to recognize the obvious, as well as the subtle signs that one of your personal boundaries has been breached:

- Have you ever been with someone who seems to pull on your energy?
- Do you feel tired whenever you spend time with a certain individual?
- Is there someone in your life who is always in crisis and looking to you not only for support, but to somehow take it on?

These are all indicators of energy leaks and drains. There are certainly times when it is appropriate to energetically support another person, like when your small child tugs at your energy (what mother hasn't felt that) or when he needs your attentive guidance. On the other hand, carrying a co-worker emotionally or energetically on a daily basis is most likely an inappropriate use of your energy. Discerning the difference is vital here, so you can plug any unnecessary leaks and know when it's time to cut someone off from the energetic feeding tube. You can learn to choose when and with whom you share your energy, and in that way, you will increase your personal vitality.

Teachers from a variety of disciplines share techniques for monitoring and clearing your energetic field. To learn more, seek out a teacher or mentor to work with individually. You can also refer to my practical meditation CD, *Spinning the Light*, which leads you through a guided experience of this transformational practice.

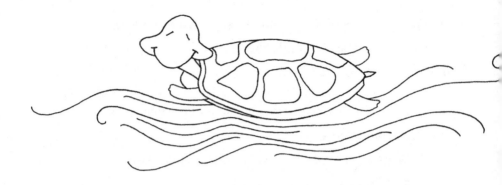

It is imperative to healthy living in our world today, that we be more conscious about the energy we put out and the energy we absorb. Like powerful Vibrational Purifiers, we sort and filter anything incongruent. We can learn to transform any negativity that we take on and release it as something better, something greater. The addition of transformed, heightened energy can positively shift our environment, too. As we change the nature of our vibration, it can be a catalyst for physical transformation all around us. It is a powerful method for affecting ourselves, our interpersonal relationships, and ultimately our planet. Fascinating!

So, what has happened to our turtle? Can you still see her meandering through the garden?

There is a stunning garden in Green Valley, Arizona, that not only contains the cactus varieties that are signature to this desert landscape, but also holds delightfully green and lovingly cared for trees and shrubs thought to be found in much moister climates.

Mesmerizing water features ensure this spot as a haven on even the hottest of days—a gentle gurgling fountain and a babbling brook winding along a meandering path with so many different types of flora that the eye doesn't know which way to look. Yet, I saw something moving in the brown underbrush, "Is that a rock?" Only when it emerged from its over-covering did I realize that this was a beautiful desert box turtle moving around in this village garden. Unexpectedly delightful. I watched her as she made her way along familiar paths, seemingly undisturbed by her fellow garden visitors. This is the place she calls home. I later learned that she just showed up one day, a gift from a friend of a friend who rescued her. She initially was to stay only while her caretaker was out of town, but she liked it here so much that everyone concerned decided to let her stay. She chose the garden, and the garden chose her!

Our metaphoric turtle is still here, too. Turtle Wisdom says when life happens, we meet it, respond to it, and learn from it. We feel its impact. Yet as things shift and change around us, we remain whole. Any one person or thing may help grow us, but nothing firmly molds us. All external energy is considered, and either rejected or accepted for its alignment with our own personal authentic core. Many things happen to us but we alone have the final say as to what shapes our lives.

Our personal authentic core
remains whole as it evolves.

~ Turtle Wisdom

Let's continue our consideration of the elements that nourish our inner garden and how we might optimize them for our most beneficial and rewarding self-expression.

Watering—Life Enrichment

> I think my lesson this time is self-care.
> I've had nourishment barriers due to my early trauma.
> Now, I'm learning to let my good in.
>
> ~ Tawni

We need to be revitalized. To give and give without renewal can leave you ragged and depleted. What depletes you? Situations that are stressful and taxing to one person can be stimulating, exciting, and quite doable for someone else. Observe what drains your energy and minimize its impact by drawing in the balance of what replenishes you.

What restores your vitality like a cool glass of water on a hot summer's day? For some, nourishment can be found by just being outside in nature, sitting under a tree or swimming in the ocean. Others go dancing and laugh with abandon, feeling free and easy with life. Whether it is a hot bath, a good book, or a fine meal, allow yourself to taste the sweetness of your favorite, simple pleasures to ensure that you remain vitally charged and ready for all that life offers.

You can't keep giving and giving without receiving. That isn't good for anyone. There is a universal principle that encourages energy to travel in a circle to find completion. It is lovingly spoken about as the Sacred Hoop of giving and receiving or the law of reciprocity. Even the most drought resistant plants require some water. Often the most delicate flowers need to be tended daily. At some point you must make yourself and your personal needs a priority and take time to recharge. You cannot just keep giving and giving and giving. Even the Eveready Energizer Bunny eventually runs out of steam. If you're already proficient in this area of finding a healthy balance, good. If not, take it on as a challenge to learn the sacred art of self-care. Refer to In the Moment (chapter 6, page 89) for a useful technique.

Weeding—Clearing

Once you've planted, you'll need to revisit your plot many times for what may be choking out your new growth. Clear the debris, getting rid of what no longer serves a useful role in your life, thereby creating space for what is alive to have room to breathe. Clearing the "weeds" opens the path for your new growth.

Some weeds are resistant and need to be literally dug out a bit at a time. Others release easily, like those grasped with a steadfast hand and pulled purposefully after a long spring rain. Those invaders let go—roots and all—gliding easily into oblivion.

Some weeds may be exceptionally persistent. I had a big barrel in my front yard with a few spikes of decorative grass framing colorful flowers to welcome guests to my front door. No matter how often I cleared it, the weeds seemed to dominate the flowers. So I covered the barrel with black plastic and let it bake with the sun's rays, deprived it of nurturing rain, and left it unattended for over a year. When I finally uncovered it, the weeds appeared to be gone, but in a very short time, there they were again, growing up from their dormancy in the soil. I had to take a drastic step by literally digging out the entire bucket to get at those roots, so I could clear the space for what I chose to plant. This is an important consideration for our personal "weeds."

To be honest, I probably would have left those weeds alone and gladly give them their turf, except for one very important fact—**weeds are invasive**, and can overtake the entire yard.

What is running rampant in your garden? What have you tried to cover up that is lying dormant under the surface? Ignoring old issues or festering wounds without addressing them does not make them go away. Given the opportunity they may sprout, emerging once again in your life.

Seek out those pesky weeds and gently remove them by getting to their root. Getting to the root and resolving them may take time. There are many modalities that can guide you through this beneficial task. Reach out if you need help.

As any gardener knows,
there will always be weeds and clearing to do.
So, make it a part of your regular practice
to see what no longer serves you in a
healthy way and dispose of it properly.
Open up your garden and let the sun
shine on your new growth.

~ Turtle Wisdom

Weeds & Seeds

One person's weeds are another person's seeds. Some people have looked in my garden and said, "Oh, that is a weed!" To me, it is a beautiful flower. My gardener tells me that some plants, which are considered noxious weeds in one environment, will be sold as flowers in another region. In those areas the seasons provide a natural control which tells these plants to rest, ensuring that they do not become invasive.

It is our job to sort the destructive or undesirable weeds from the significant seeds ...

- When concerns, worries, insecurities, and fears surface, discern how relevant they are for you now.
- Does this understandably relate to the current situation or is this a pattern that was somehow ingrained in you from an earlier time?
- Ask yourself if it is really what is true for you.

For instance, many people have told a similar story of being raised by parents of the depression, who constantly worried about money and collected large stores of canned goods and toilet paper "just in case." And what about the infamous "toilet paper shortage" and resulting hysteria during the 2020 pandemic? People fret about money even though they have successful careers and more than enough to provide for their families. Sometimes this fear is relative to much earlier experiences, especially those from their impressionable childhood. We call it our "family of origin" for a reason—much of our early conditioning originates there. There may be attitudes, beliefs, and philosophies that you have outgrown, that you no longer believe, but they still somehow impact your behavior or have influence over you.

- What is your origin story? Where did you come from? What was your family like?
- What were your early experiences? How did they help shape the lens through which you view the world?
- In what situations do you notice your early conditioning showing up? You may see it in one area of your life, but not others.
- What patterns still influence you?
- When you react to something, ask yourself, "how old do I feel?" Sometimes that can give you a clue to where its roots lie.

You can take this contemplation even further. When a circumstance arises, identify whether how you react or what feelings arise give you clues to what's going on beneath the surface. What can you learn from it? Therein may be a potential seed for your growth.

- What happens when you examine your reaction?
- What understanding can you bring forth?
- Has this behavior ever served a purpose?
- Does it now serve you in some manner?
- What can you do to improve the situation?
- If necessary, how can you rectify it? Or how can you alter your reaction?
- What possibilities are there for new growth?

On the other hand, if you notice that your immediate reaction is not warranted by the outer picture or your personal beliefs as they are now, but is somehow an old, outgrown, ineffective pattern still alive, seek out its destructive, limiting roots. Pull forth that nasty bindweed, freeing your garden from the space it occupies, and opening it to the light of day. No longer do you allow it to choke off your vital growth. No longer does it impact your success or happiness.

> This is not a one-time venture! Your thoughtful consideration and conscious weeding are both an ongoing endeavor. As this practice continues, your attention to it minimizes what depletes you and maximizes what encourages your grandest blossoms.

An old Native American story speaks
of a grandfather counseling his grandson.
He tells the boy that he has two wolves inside of him
struggling with each other for dominance.
The first is the wolf of kindness, peace, and love.
The other is the wolf of greed, fear, and hatred.
The wide-eyed boy asks, "Which wolf will win, grandfather?"

The grandfather wisely replies,
"Whichever one I feed."

Fertilizing—"Old Shit" Makes Good Manure!

Life is like photography ... we use the negative to develop.

~ Henry Cohen Baba

Does your smile feel inauthentic? If you tend to insincerely put forward a positive face, you might miss the point. You need to first identify what is "crap." Acknowledge it for what it is—in whatever words work best for you. Because if you sugarcoat the crap ... well, it's still crap. It's powerful to call it out for what it is. Once you've identified it, you don't have to stay stuck in it. Your wide-eyed awareness allows you to move through it and to transform it into something else. Like richly seasoned fertilizer this old, sometimes smelly stuff, can be quite helpful; you can use it to nourish your new growth.

All the stuff of our past difficult experiences—our trials and tribulations, the pain we felt, the emotions we've grieved, the lessons we've learned —are rich nutrients for the fertile soil of our growth. Just like a fine quality manure, they may add, rather than take away from our ability to thrive. When you see something you don't like about your past or your present, remember that you possess the ability to change it. And the spoils of that evolutionary process will be a useful addition to your garden.

If we truly draw forward and integrate the meaning of where we have come from and what we have experienced, if we allow that richness to sink deep into the soil, then we honor those times, good or bad. We utilize every useful part of those experiences and we benefit from their existence.

Affirm:
CaCa be Gone!
CaCa Transform

Growing and Evolving

People have said to me, "I have been working on myself for  years now. When will it end?" NEVER! (I hope!) While you have another breath to take, hopefully, you will be growing, stretching, exploring in new ways, and refining who you are as an individual, unique creation. When my son was young, I stitched a wall hanging for his room which served as a reminder to me, "Be Patient. God isn't finished with me yet." And neither is She (He) finished with you.

You are an evolving human being; be gentle with yourself through all the changes. Like the flowers in the garden, understand that every one of your phases has merit. Celebrate all your experiences, not just your successes ... for together, they help you stretch wide as you open to the sun.

You are Beauty Blossoming

Are you holding back? Are you keeping part of your individuality from being expressed? Are there hidden qualities you stifle? Perhaps you are shy about displaying your true self or perhaps you lack the confidence to believe in the value of what it is that you have to show. What is surprising to me is that even the most gifted people often ask the question, "Who am I to do that?" or "Why, me?" What separates those who bring their talents through to fruition and those who don't, isn't the level of their capacity, but rather the level of commitment to try and see what is possible.

When we clear the weeds of self-doubt and plant "can-do" seeds of assurance, we are more apt to experiment with what lies dormant within us. What would life be like if you took those qualities out, dusted them off and lived from that perspective? We limit ourselves by what we imagine is true.

> **There is so much more to you than even you know!**
> You may have a metaphoric greenhouse
> full of rare orchids waiting to be seen.

Be courageously, authentically "you." Act genuinely, sincerely aligned with your intentions; vulnerable, yet protected, so you might share who you truly are on the inside with those around you. Let your light shine and sparkle in the outside world.

- Believe in yourself and in your gifts, talents, and abilities.
- Recognize the areas in which you are blossoming, as well as those that need your attention to grow.
- Acknowledge life in its natural progression, unfolding rightfully, moment by moment to help you become more of the person you can be.
- Be open to glimmers of your yet-unexpressed potential, let the sun of your awareness shine upon them, illuminating them, and bringing them to life.
- Nurture elements of acceptance, trust, and peace in your daily living.
- Realize that everything has meaning and purpose.

Would you ever see a sunflower wishing it was a daffodil?

Open more fully to receive the understanding of the gift that you are and learn to express from the fullness of what you possess. You are remarkable! And we need the part that you can contribute. Without you and your unique harvest, our shared sustenance would be incomplete.

Be yourself.
Everyone else is already taken.

~ Anonymous

Genuinely show who you are to the world. Be real.

"What is Real?" asked Rabbit one day, when they were lying side by side near the nursery fender, before Nana came to tidy the room.

"Does it mean having things that buzz inside you and a stick-out handle?"

"Real isn't how you are made," said the Skin Horse. "It's a thing that happens to you. When a child loves you for a long, long time, not just to play with, but REALLY loves you, then you become Real."

"Does it hurt?" asked Rabbit.

"Sometimes," said the Skin Horse, for he was always truthful. "When you are Real you don't mind being hurt."

"Does it happen all at once, like being wound up," he asked, "or bit by bit?"

"It doesn't happen all at once," said the Skin Horse. "You become. It takes a long time. That's why it doesn't often happen to people who break easily, or have sharp edges, or have to be carefully kept. Generally, by the time you are Real, most of your hair has been loved off, and your eyes drop out and you get loose in the joints and very shabby. But these things don't matter at all, because once you are Real you can't be ugly, except to people who don't understand."

~ Margery Williams, *The Velveteen Rabbit*

> Happiness is not a state to arrive at,
> but a manner of traveling.
>
> – Margaret Lee Runbeck

Share your bounty with the world around you. Give the gift of your authentic, sincere character ... and allow that sincerity to provide nourishment to help sustain us all. You are a part of life itself. We all need what you have to offer. I can't wait to see what you bring to our collective table so we might partake in a grand feast!

One final note here in our Growing and Evolving section: in the last chapter, I mentioned being an earth guardian by recognizing that we not only walk upon the earth, but we are a part of her and she is a part of us. It is our human responsibility to be aware of our treatment of her and to live in a manner which respects and honors our planet; we have been entrusted with her care. My Peruvian teachers taught me the concept of "Ayni" (pronounced "i-nee"), which is the sacred law of reciprocity. We do not take without giving back ... and we are attentive to each other's needs. Be conscious of what you do and remember to walk gently upon the earth, so she may thrive for future generations. Be a sustainable part of our overall greater "home," our dear planet.

Connect with the earth beneath you and the wildness within you. Your untamed inner space holds the potential to shift your present state of being, to buck stuck paradigms, and to create anew. Go beyond your intellect, into vast spaces of heart and soul.

Be mindful of what you put into the world. Your thoughts, words, and actions plant seeds for the future. Caring for them is one powerful way you can tend to the soul of the world.

> A society grows great
> when old men plant trees
> whose shade they know they shall never sit in.
>
> ~ *A Greek proverb*

Nature's Wisdom

> To everything there is a season,
> a time for every purpose under the sun.
> A time to be born and a time to die.
> A time to plant, and a time
> to pluck up that which is planted ...
>
> ~ *Ecclesiastes:3:1*

Everything has value in nature, the smallest blade of grass to the greatest redwood has its rightful place in our ecosystem at every stage of their development. The cycles of life create through us just as they do in the outer, natural world. We can trust the wisdom of each stage of our growth, just as we can appreciate the evolving stages of a garden—the seed, the sprout, the bud, the blossom, the deadhead, and the return to the earth.

Nature has wisdom and knows when to adapt. There is a strength and tenacity which is innate and self-evident. What about the trees that grow through rocks or the tiny weeds which find their homes in cracks of walkways? That same tenacity and will to survive pulses through your being. You are strong and resilient.

Greatness lives in you, too, like the potential in the seed. Just as a vast garden has tremendous variety, you, too, have many colors, shapes, and textures to express your natural impulse. Go ahead and broaden your vision, as you encourage the variations of your innate beauty to burst forth! Like caring for seeds, you need to feed, fertilize, and water your inner garden to enable it to grow. You must nurture your potential and then delight in its blossoming. There is a potential within you that is beyond your wildest dreams—and in the proper environment you will thrive. No matter what you encounter or what you are called to do, you always have "you." So, come home to yourself and then, when needed, you can re-parent, partner, or befriend yourself. Believe in yourself and *everything that is within you* is possible.

> To be of the Earth is to know
> the restlessness of being a seed
> the darkness of being planted
> the struggle toward the light
> the pain of growth into the light
> the joy of bursting and bearing fruit
> the love of being food for someone
> the scattering of your seeds
> the decay of the seasons
> the mystery of death
> and the miracle of birth.
>
> *~ John Soos*

There is so much more to you than even you know!

Part II

5

Coming of Age:
Recognizing All That You Are

> I was always looking outside myself for strength and confidence,
> but it comes from within. It is there all the time.
>
> ~ Anna Freud

I don't think fear limits people as much as the deep underlying belief that they do not deserve love/happiness/success. I wonder what it would be like if we never had a notion that in some way, shape, or form we are not good enough. No thoughts of not being smart enough, attractive enough or clever enough. No feelings of being too this or too that. Not even a fleeting sense of insecurity. What would that be like? ... What does "good enough" look like? What does "good enough" feel like?

- Do you often seek approval to validate how you feel about yourself?
- Are you looking for reassurance from someone or something?
- What are you looking for—really?

- You know, when a woman is in a certain mood, she can receive 50 compliments and one criticism ... What will she hear? She'll often be riveted to the one criticism, letting it penetrate her deeply, like an arrow through her heart, whether it is constructive or not.

When someone makes a comment, I find it helpful to evaluate how relevant it is for me. I process the words, feelings, and sentiment behind the statement through my own filters. His perspective may be truthful or valid from his point of view and yet be downright outrageous from mine. These things are honestly quite subjective.

> Once at a retreat I was facilitating, a participant complimented me on a meditation I led saying it was very moving and inspirational. She also relayed, "At one point, you said the word 'but' and do you realize that when you say 'but,' it negates what you said previously?" I believe her comment was well intentioned—BUT the fact is when I lead a guided meditation, I am in the flow of inspiration. I do not preplan nor script them. If I censored every word, it would interrupt the natural flow and grace of the meditation. Her perspective, regardless of how valid it was, was not useful for me. If I had interpreted it as a criticism, it might have been defeating. And yet, her reflection had value for me. I am grateful for it as the catalyst to explore the dynamics in and through those kinds of comments. Perhaps in another case, I might have taken a similar one more personally and been hurt or used it as motivation to alter my approach. In this instance, what I do works for me, so although she had a valid point, it did not fit into my larger framework.

Quite simply, most of the time, people are just voicing their opinions. Their impression is seen through their filters and is only describing that idea from their vantage point. One comment does not solidify the reality for anyone else—unless you allow it to do so. Even in the cases where someone has authority over you, like in a work situation, what they see about you may not be the truth of who you are, and you must know that their words do not have ultimate dominion over you. How you interpret their observations and internalize their comments holds all the power. Instead of being defeated by negative assessments, if you can take them in and extract what is useful to help you grow, they will be most beneficial.

> When we seek approval outside of ourselves to validate us or take other's opinions in too deeply, we give those people and their perspectives power. Comments may weaken our self-esteem and cause us to question ourselves, thereby making us more self-conscious. If we allow them to, these criticisms can impair our natural and spontaneous expression, lessen our joy, and in some cases even devastate us. Other people's opinions do not define you—unless you allow them to do so. Don't buy into them unless they are meaningful to you because when you take those comments on, they can weigh you down, impairing your ability to fly. And even a turtle cannot move forward if he's carrying too much weight on his shell.
>
> Remember, no one can make you feel inferior without your consent.
>
> *~ Eleanor Roosevelt*

Your personal boundaries are solid, yet permeable, letting in pertinent and helpful information, but keeping out hurtful, non-productive input. Like rain on a turtle's shell, a critical irrelevant comment can just roll right off your back!

One important thing to consider is that you must build your confidence from the inside out—not the other way around. Recognize that **the center of your worthiness is within you**. You can remain unshakable even when you make mistakes or don't know how to do something; those potential energy leaks do not destructively drain your sense of self. If you do not love yourself, no matter how much others love you, it will never be enough. It's like having your confidence and self-esteem held captive in an ever-present sieve: you lose the love and appreciation through those unpluggable holes just as fast as it is given.

Picture an infinitely deep dark hole—filling it would be unfathomable—even reaching the outer edges would take a lifetime. Some of us harbor that kind of deep crevice and attempt to fill it with outer validation. No matter how much you gather and dump in there, the cavernous crater never seems to fill to the top where confidence lives. Instead, the insecurities that are harbored there bounce back to us and reverberate into our outer reality.

For that matter, some people take to heart any negative comments, while resisting any compliments or gestures of appreciation. Sometimes it's because they've had good reasons for learning to distrust people. Or perhaps it's because their hefty sense of unworthiness negates any positivity that's directed toward them.

- Do you block the good that tries to come your way?
- Do positive comments make you uncomfortable? Do they just stir up the murky bottom of insecurity within you, sending it whirling?
- Although we mustn't base our security and sense of self on what comes to us from the outside, it is helpful to hear and consider positive comments.
- Ultimately, it is you who must sort what's useful from what's not.
- It is you who must cultivate your self-worth and nurture your self-esteem.

> Dismantling the old "me,"
> I decide to do no harm—and that includes me.
> Letting in the "good" gives me so many choices.
> I accept that everyone deserves good—
> and that includes me.
>
> ~ Tawni

Notice when someone compliments you or appreciates your achievements:

- What happens to your body?
- Are you able to hold eye contact and feel the impact of their appreciation?
- Or do your shoulders sink in to shield your heart and keep their kind words out?
- Do your eyes shift to the floor or gaze past the person speaking goodness to you? Are you unable to connect ... and receive?

Observe yourself the next time someone offers you a compliment and notice your natural reaction. It is a guidepost to your innermost feelings and beliefs.

Even if you can let appreciation in, do you truly accept and internalize it? Or does the mind chatter begin negating the loving words as soon as they move toward you? "Sure, I did that well, but I am not really that capable. I couldn't accomplish that other task yesterday. I got stuck mid-stream." That kind of mental muddle is not constructive, it's destructive. That's a **worthiness leak!**

Return once again to your authentic core and your relationship with yourself. If you cultivate a security based on your own love and appreciation, then when someone adds to that understanding, it will warm the very cockles of your heart. You don't need them to validate who you are, their words simply add to your intact center. Your confidence emerges and develops into a strong, resilient core which allows you to express yourself freely from your own authenticity, with an understanding that how you express and what you share may not be everyone's cup of tea.

You can receive compliments and criticisms in the same vein. Neutrally. You don't need compliments to build you up, nor do the criticisms tear you down. It is simply INFORMATION, and you can receive it as such. Perhaps it helps you better shape your future by helping to alter or refine you in some way. Or you might simply receive it, process it, and release it for it has no relevance to your way of being.

I keep the telephone of my mind open
to peace, harmony, health, love, and abundance.
Then whenever doubt, anxiety, or fear try to call me,
they keep getting a busy signal
and soon they'll forget my number.

~ Edith Armstrong

Unshakable
in my core foundation
nurtured
by the very nature
of who I am.

~ Turtle Wisdom

Physical Beauty

Things that matter most must never be at the mercy
of things which matter least.

~ Goethe

A long time ago, I knew a man who had been married to a strikingly beautiful woman. Even so, for other reasons, there were problems. Since this was in my early adulthood and I had never been totally at ease with my physical appearance, I was really struck by his comment that he had been with "a gorgeous woman with a knock-out body and yet he was surprised at how ugly she could be." Wow! I was

73

moved by his verbalization of what is commonly known yet not always demonstrated, that beauty is more than skin deep. At certain times, this woman's behavior caused her to appear unattractive despite how physically stunning she was.

I have witnessed well-paid fashion models dissect their looks, obsessing over what they consider the most minute "flaw." Just because someone is considered beautiful by society standards does not assure that she is confident about herself. And of course, many of us contest the idea of any standard of beauty arguing that each one has and expresses beauty in our own unique ways. I certainly believe that now!

It's interesting to note that even in what is often considered a very superficially driven society, physical beauty doesn't seem to be the strongest driving force for attraction. One sociological study followed successful models and what was deemed "plain" women into a social setting and observed how their behavior influenced the way men related to them. Time and time again, it was observed that each woman's behavior, not her physical beauty, determined attractiveness. Men were drawn to the approachable, vivacious, and engaging women, whereas the beautiful, aloof women sat alone. Body language communicated strong messages in these situations. When the unapproachable women altered their behavior to make them more accessible, their desirability shifted. How these women interacted with the men was the single most important factor to their popularity, not physical beauty.

Another contributing factor of how we relate regarding the physical level is that sometimes people shy away from what's radically different because there is an illusion of "other" that separates individuals unnecessarily. Someone may be set apart because of an aspect or quality that unfortunately isn't responded to well or treated kindly.

> There was a time when I was so different that I stuck out like a sore thumb. And that's a good description, too, because I sure did ache. My family moved to a new town, and I changed from the Catholic school I had attended for six years to a new public school. I went from wearing uniforms every day and looking like everyone else in my class to being thrown into an environment where status was determined, at least partially, by what you wore. And I had three outfits! That's not even enough for a different look each day of the school week. My parents were providing new clothes for four children at the time, and those three outfits were all they could afford. It sealed my fate.
>
> I was singled out in the harshness of seventh grade as an easy target and terrorized for the whole year. Lunchtime was the worst when kids bullied me without the watchful eyes of teachers who were restfully tucked away in the teacher lounge. My classmates taunted me with nasty names, some I won't repeat here. "Dog" wasn't a cleverly cruel comment, but when it's chanted by a group of girls throwing hard milk bones at your head, well, that hurts.

Many of us have a time or a place when we didn't fit in—a time and a place where we were singled out cruelly. When we remember those details and how horrible it felt, that insight helps us show empathy toward others who are being attacked or ostracized. And gratefully, at this time in our societal evolution, we are now examining the deeper issues of prejudice and entitlement, and the impacts of those distorted lenses and woundings upon our world. Hopefully those times of your own challenges around being misunderstood, judged, or set apart may inspire you to show kindness to others who are different from you ... and even more importantly, to celebrate those differences.

One story of remarkable courage is that of Jacqueline Saburido, a special kind of hero.

> On September 19, 1999, Jacqui, a stunningly beautiful 20-year-old woman, had a promising lifetime ahead of her. On that fateful day, she was a passenger in a car with four other women on the outskirts of Austin, Texas when they were hit by an 18-year-old high school student on his way home from drinking with friends. He was less than a mile from his driveway when his car drifted across the road and struck the girls' car head on, killing two of Jacqui's friends. As the car caught fire, two others were pulled alive from the burning wreck, but she remained inside for nearly a minute before first responders were able to put the flames out and extract her. Jacqui Saburido received third-degree burns over 60% of her body and was left severely disfigured. Her previously flawless face was now unrecognizable.
>
> Called "the woman who was burned alive," Jacqueline became a moving spokesperson of numerous drunk-driving campaigns and even appeared on the Oprah Show recounting her unthinkable story in devastating detail. Yet, despite all she went through, Jacqui was a vibrant, loving woman who held no grudge against the young man who was responsible for the crash. He was convicted on two counts of intoxication manslaughter and sentenced to seven years in prison, where

he collaborated with Saburido on an anti-DWI campaign after she told him she forgave him.

Listening to her share her story in great detail was like a smack in the face, it stung long after the initial impact. And yet, in contrast, it was greatly impactful how loving and accepting Jacqui was and how she had come to terms with all she had gone through. Many people exclaimed how beautiful she was—and within her badly disfigured face and body there was an undeniably bright light, which radiated extraordinary beauty.

"Even if it means sitting here in front of a camera with no ears, no nose, no eyebrows, no hair, I'll do this a thousand times if it will help someone make a wise decision," Jacqueline Saburido said during one of her many press appearances. Jacqui spent the rest of her lifetime campaigning for alcohol-free driving and to this day, remains an enduring symbol of what it means to be truly beautiful.

We are each unique. Recognizing beauty in all its forms doesn't mean ignoring its differences. Jacqueline was beautiful despite her horrific disfigurement. Part of our growth can be growing past seeing only the physical and being able to see and value what else is there. But that doesn't mean we need to totally ignore the physical either.

When I was a young single working mother studying at Cornell University in Ithaca, New York, I was juggling many roles. It became necessary one day to take my five-year-old son by the hand and head up the steep hill onto campus. I couldn't miss an important class on this day when his school for gifted children was closed. So, with his little backpack filled with projects to keep him busy, we took a seat in the back of the room that was filled with rows of old-fashioned school desks—you know the wooden ones with the tabletop and seat attached. Just as the professor entered the classroom, I realized Todd had slipped down and away from his seat and was standing purposefully in front of a woman in the front row center.

"Why do you have blind eyes?" he asked matter-of-factly in a loud voice. Jennie's broad smile lit up her entire face. And just as matter-of-factly, she told him her whole story. Astounding. None of us knew, not even the professor, that she wasn't born blind, but became so through illness. We had been classmates with Jennie for over a year, but out of some awkward politeness, no one had asked about what was considered a disability. It took this bright child with a genuine curiosity for us to learn the truth. And through her story, we gained a greater respect and appreciation for her. I also realized just how special my open, inquisitive, and accepting child was and is—he certainly was life's classroom teacher that day.

> We know what we are,
> but not what we may be.
>
> ~ William Shakespeare

I strive to be kind and compassionate,
a good friend, and an interesting person.
Now on a bad hair day, I focus on what really matters and let my light shine through.

Say "Yes" to your own unique beauty even when you have a zit on your chin, and don't be surprised if no one else even notices!

> The future belongs to those who believe
> in the beauty of their dreams.
>
> ~ *Eleanor Roosevelt*

Sometimes one small gift from another can be the very thing that's necessary to help you shift and catapult you on a new path; one small thing to help you come of age and recognize all that you are. When I was going through a messy divorce, I felt lost and alone, unsure where to turn. Although I had good friends, I thought no-one understood the hurt and pain I was feeling. I stumbled upon an affirmation that was the beacon of light to guide me through the darkness that clouded my vision. It was the comfort and understanding I needed to see me through. Unfortunately, I have never been able to identify the origin of this detailed affirmation (that came my way long before affirmations were fashionable). This affirmation is one I've held dear for almost fifty years! I share it now with respect, appreciation, and gratitude for the person who created it. If you are reading my words, reach out to me. I have a big hug with your name on it.

To encourage your ability to recognize and embrace the fullness of your beauty, repeat the following affirmation out loud for twenty-one days.

Affirmation of the Unlimited Person

I am powerful and able. I am successful.
I am whole and complete.
The Universe supports me.
My body is filled with energy and vitality.
I am light. I am buoyant.
Natural wellbeing flows through me.
All I deserve is in reach.
I am powerful, attractive, and wealthy.
Abundance is my birthright.
This I manifest now.

I forgive myself. Today I begin life anew.
Joy and love flow from me as from a fountain.
Love is in my heart as I meet each situation.
Love is in my heart as I meet each person.
I move out into the world with love.
I am discovering this now.

I am persistent. I have tenacity.
The will to succeed supports me totally.
Barriers become my education.
I experience obstacles as opportunities,
which lie on my path to success.

I am confident. The power of the Universe
manifests Itself through me now.
My actions are decisive.
I walk in power and affirmation of life ...

~ Author Unknown

Awakening a Masterful Life—
One of Your Very Own Design

If we did all the things we are capable of,
we would literally astound ourselves.

~ Thomas Edison

> Life isn't about finding yourself—about discovering
> your perfect career or marrying the love of your life.
> Life is about creating yourself by drawing forward the very best
> of who you are; and shaping and reshaping yourself
> in alignment with your essential core, that unique part
> of you that is your most "you" you!

I've said it before, but I'll say it again, there is so much more to you than even you know. **"Coming of Age" signifies that you truly see yourself** for the totality of who are. It is a call to recognize the depth and the breadth of your being; to see that you were born for a reason, or perhaps for many, many reasons. You are unique and precious. There is no one else like you. You are absolutely worthy of all the goodness life can offer and all the greatness you can achieve.

Recognize that there is not one perfect destiny for you, but many possibilities along the way.

Your life path need not be determined by what you are good at doing, nor by what someone else decides you should do. There are significant moments which potentially shape your future, and in those moments, you can make choices born of your desires.

Reach high; for stars lie hidden in your soul
Dream deep, for every dream precedes the goal.

~ Pamela Vaull Starr

Goodness Ripples Forward

As you fully claim, and step into the personal power to affect your own life, you become a positive influence on those around you. Empowered living enables you to discern situations and engage with people from a place of accountability and maturity; you do not blame others for what happens to you, but rather find the meaning and purpose in the experiences that come your way. You actively engage in your life in a manner which is co-creative and directive, helping to shape your future. You recognize the value in all people and all life experiences and by your example, others may be inspired to recognize and enrich their own preciousness, too.

This empowered, positive vibration moves out like a tuning fork in ever widening circles, as you become a contributor toward a healing shift in our collective consciousness. As you come of age, you recognize just how much external impact you can have. You show up mindfully and act purposefully in a way that can uplift those around you ... and beyond. You are a beneficial presence. And you hold the vision of our culture moving past those destructive, limiting beliefs that constrain our worldly reality and instead stretch toward an evolved, heightened state of living.

Breathe deeply. Reach inside and pull forth your best self. Accept the potential you have been endowed with and make your individuality the very best that it can be.

Be fully alive!

Embrace Life!

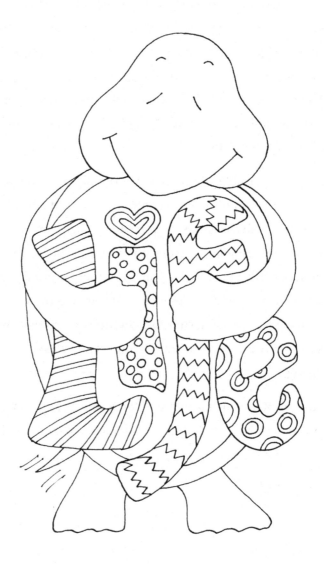

6

In the Moment

*The secret of health for both body and mind
is to live in the present moment wisely and earnestly.*

~ Buddha

Have you ever noticed someone not being present to what he is doing in the moment? "The lights are on, but no one is home!" We are all guilty of it from time to time. Someone is talking and our mind wanders elsewhere; we bump into the wall going round the corner because we're not seeing where we are going, but instead focused on the task ahead; the toothpaste goes in the freezer and the ice cream in the medicine chest! With all the responsibilities of the day weighing on us, it is understandable that we are preoccupied.

Yet, there is a sweetness to being in the moment, a relief to letting go of everything else and focusing on the here and now. You will never have this moment again—and whatever is happening is significant and holds meaning. If you are oblivious to it, you might miss that point. When you turn your acute awareness to your individual moments, life takes on a richer sweetness. If you are looking ahead ... or behind, you miss the importance of Now. Be here, now. Be more present; be more conscious. Drink in your experience, swallowing every last drop. Totally immerse yourself and swim in it. This is not a dress rehearsal; this is your life. You will never have *this* moment again. Live it!

If we consider life as a production—a play, a movie, a grand adventure—are you the script writer, the producer, the director, the lead, or simply a supporting cast member? Honestly, you are all those roles at various times, but be sure you accept the lead role in your own life.

Some people wait for life to happen to them, poised for the challenges and successes it may bring. And when those challenges or successes come, they react to what's set before them, dealing with it the best they can by following the trail where it leads. They take the script that's been given them and do their best to pour their heart and soul into it, hopeful of a winning performance.

Others take a more pro-active stance. They grab life by the hand and encourage it to move down a chosen path, or perhaps encourage it to travel deep into the uncharted wood, or invite it to dance delightfully in a field of wildflowers. These seekers actively engage with life, squeezing the juice right out of it; savoring its sweetness, and licking their lips to take in every last bit. These are the script writers, actively designing what they imagine possible; the producers investing in their chosen direction; and then, they step right into the lead, bringing their ideas into action while helping to direct the story as it unfolds. Everything might not be within their control, but they masterfully orchestrate what is within their circle of influence. They are fully engaged with life.

Notice what makes you happy ... and what does not. Be aware of what drains your energy ... and what puts a pep in your step! Observe what efforts return to you successfully ... and when they do not. With your earnest attention to your daily living, you can shape and reshape what you're pursuing and how you are doing so—to assure that you are living your very best through the conscious choices you make.

By taking what is given and claiming it as your own, you can sculpt it into what you'd like it to be. It's impressive how much you can accomplish when you actively assume the nuances of your character. After all, it is your very own wisdom story. And by being present to your moments, you can optimize your health, wealth, and happiness.

Let your outer world reflect your inner vision: the truest pathways stretch from your heart and soul to dreams come true.

~ Donna DeNomme

Good Morning, Sunshine

Write on your heart that every day is the best day of the year.

~ Ralph Waldo Emerson

Awaken to each new day with anticipation as if it was your birthday and today, you'll be receiving many gifts. Some may even be quite unexpected like stumbling into a surprise party!

When you greet the day in this manner, you establish an energetic field that attracts goodness to you. You expect ... and then accept ... goodness.

For we honestly do receive gifts every day, yet many slip by unnoticed because we are so distracted by our daily activities. Recognize the kind words of a co-worker, the infectious smile of a child, the quarter you find on the street corner, or the sun playing peek-a-boo behind a cloud. As you savor this sweetness, you set up a field of receiving that grows and re-seeds itself. Every day is filled with wonderment.

Pull out all the stops! Open the space for a richer expression and expand in ever-widening circles. Risk. Explore. Expect and accept all the gifts that come your way. Believe in miracles. Then, life might surprise you with even more-than-you-expected good! Life truly can be a glorious adventure when you let go of your small attachments and open to the greater possibilities of what might be.

> Psychologist and spiritual teacher Ram Dass tells a well known story about the way you catch a monkey in India. You place a handful of nuts into a jar with a small opening and leave it nearby. The monkey puts his hand into the jar, grabs the nuts, and tries to pull them out through the small opening. He refuses to release his hold on the nuts, which keeps his hand stuck in the jar. If he let go of the nuts, he would be able to remove his hand and escape. His attachment to what's in his hand leads to his capture.

How often do you behave as the monkey, unable to let go of what you hold tightly in your hand? If you did so, might it lead to you being able to escape an undesirable condition or a destructive situation? Is this the path to greater freedom?

> You are holding a cactus plant in your hand. You are bleeding and cursing the cactus but not letting go of it. Cactus is not hurting you. Your own attachment with the cactus is hurting you.
>
> ~ *Shunya*

> To let go does not mean to get rid of. To let go means to let be.
> When we let be with compassion, things come and go on their own.
>
> *~ Jack Kornfield*
>
> When I let go of what I am, I become what I might be.
>
> *~ Lao Tzu*

So, we learn how to let go of attachments, how to surrender, and how to trust the process of our becoming. On the other hand, we must also consider how we can embrace ourselves and how we can give ourselves what we need.

Self-Care is Essential

How do you care for yourself? Self-Care is important for cultivating your happiness and well-being. It is not a "one and done" kind of thing, but is something that is necessary ongoing, especially in times of stress.

Self-care relates to what you do for your mental, emotional, physical, and spiritual health. It includes the basics like eating healthy, maintaining a regular sleep schedule, and getting proper exercise. It also stretches into enrichment activities like developing healthy relationships, being in nature, and doing activities that feed your heart and soul. It includes the recreational and the social. You might even include getting a massage or visiting a spa for relaxation.

Being mindful of where you are and what you need (in the moment) is essential. Neglecting self-care is simply put, not loving yourself. Self-care may look different for each one of us, but it must promote your health and happiness.

Self-care is not necessarily a natural endeavor but can be a learned behavior—one you purposely develop:

- Experts teach us that it often takes at least 21 days to create a new habit.
- Assess where you are right now with your self-care. Also notice how you feel. Are you relaxed, rested, energized ... or frazzled, harried, drained?
- Make a list of what areas need improvement in your self-care and think about a routine that fits them into your daily schedule.
- Commit to try them faithfully for the next 21 days.
- Then reassess how you feel. At this point, you can adjust your self-care to optimize its effectiveness.
- Practice, practice, practice the sacred art of self-care. You'll fine-tune what's best for you.

> What one or two things are you doing today—just for you, your health, and your wellbeing? Strengthen your self-care understanding and your self-care commitment.

Put yourself on your to-do list! You know, you don't necessarily need to be at the very top of that list—but you must be on it ... regular, consistent self-care enriches your life and in turn, the lives of those around you. Being present to your moments enables you to notice when your self-care is slipping through the cracks. Commit to taking care of yourself.

> Better keep yourself clean and bright;
> you are the window through
> which you must see the world.
>
> *~ George Bernard Shaw*

Take the Time

Here are a few suggestions for enhancing your ability to be present in the moment as a part of your self-care:

- Find peace in solitude. Practice being at home with yourself.
- Make time to listen to your own thoughts. You might have something fascinating to say. This is important for your mental health, too—listening to the small whisper asking for help is much better than ignoring it until it turns into a blood-curdling scream. Give your precious thoughts the attention they crave.
- On the other hand, you can also take time to be in stillness—so you can let go of your thoughts, so you can be present to and then let go of your emotions, so you can sink further within, beyond thought and beyond emotion ... and open to what might be there.

> Take the time to discover the things that feed your soul. It is imperative to your physical, emotional, and spiritual health.

- Take ten minutes. Time yourself so you take a full ten minutes.
- Jot a list of endeavors you would like to pursue. These can be simple and easy-to-complete or more complex, requiring forethought and planning. Enjoy ice cream at the park while sitting under a tree. Call a friend and have a short chat. Sing with your full voice while cleaning the house. Visit ancient ruins in Greece. Take an Alaskan cruise.
- Allow yourself to write down anything that pops into your head. You can edit to refine it or delete it later if you choose to strike it from your list. Write continuously until the allotted time is up.
- Reread your list and see if there are any surprises. Add any last-minute thoughts or revisions. Keep the list handy and add to it when you are further inspired.
- Note: I often engage in this activity or offer it as a birthday process for others. You can do this by numbering a page with your birthday numbers—if you are turning 20, your number is 20. If you are turning 60, then you get 60! Nudge yourself to imagine something you'd like to have or do, and then record on each numbered line. The bonus, of course, is that the older you are the more "birthday wishes" you get to record.
- Believe you can (and will) engage in what's on your list, simply because it's something you'd like to do!!! Choose from your list whenever you can and pursue your simple pleasures and wildest interests.

Time Out

Some pursue happiness, others create it.

~ Ralph Waldo Emerson

Do you enjoy hanging out with yourself? Not exclusively, of course, but periodically taking some time out to see a movie alone, go to an unfamiliar or favorite museum, or visit a farmer's market with all the time to browse at your leisure. What a delight to go on an adventure with yourself, following your own whims and patterns, leaving early if you are finished or lingering if you desire. Experience the place, the event, and the people you encounter through your own filters and your own timing. The most ordinary endeavor, like strolling in the park or visiting a library can be a fun adventure if you fancy it as a special date with yourself. Give it the same attention you would if you were out with a loved one. Simply divine!

Unstructured Time

Have a "sunshine on your shoulders" day!

~ My friend, Cam Goodman

One way to practice personal freedom is to take a day (or a few hours if a whole day isn't possible) and allow yourself to effortlessly flow from one project to another, or from one whim to another without a specific agenda or timetable. It's a summertime-out-of-school kind of day. Include one in your schedule every week, month, or quarter— anytime you can squeeze it in. Guaranteed to recharge and renew your zest for life.

> Wisdom is found in doing
> the next thing you have to do,
> doing it with your whole heart,
> and finding delight in it.
>
> ~ *Meister Eckart, Medieval Mystic*

Mind Memory Moments

So, what about your *absolutely delightful* moments? The fleeting moments when things align in the best of ways, and you experience happiness ... or joy ... or contentment. Or perhaps you achieve something you've been striving for, working toward. What do you do in those moments? Do you pause and soak in the sweet essence of them? Or do you rush right on through to the next task in front of you?

Some of us are comfortable with those good feelings; others are not. For some, life has been wrought with mistreatment, trauma, abuse, or overwhelming challenges causing them to distrust the "good" when it comes their way. Their focus may instead be on wondering and worrying what might come next, waiting for the other shoe to drop. They just don't trust the good.

We may need to practice happiness. Even if you are able to let yourself be happy, you can still enhance your ability to accept joy or success. You can amp up your ability to *feel* what you are experiencing—to really feel it, every bit of its goodness, and to stretch that feeling so it lasts longer than just in the moment it occurs. You can repattern your brain to let go of the defense mechanisms that hold your good a hands length away ... and teach yourself instead to trust the good feeling so you might truly embrace its dear essence.

You can take that even further as you practice coding those good moments in your mind and heart, so you might "call them up" or revisit them when need be.

Learning to accept happiness is not only an individual endeavor but is our collective evolutionary growth. As we cultivate goodness, it will evolve in greater and greater circles of being, uplifting our planet. Embodying light can help tip the balance and heal the darkness in our world. And the more comfortable we are with goodness and light, the more inclined we are to share that with others, spreading goodness and light through our thoughts, words, and actions.

Here's an easy practice for those times when you want to remember a happiness, a joy, an accomplishment, or an inspiring moment, so you may call it back to you when you need a lift or a boost to empower your day.

I call them "Mind Memory Moments:"

1. Pause. Take time to notice when something is sparking joy, when something is making you happy, or when you achieve a success.
2. Be present to those moments when they are happening and savor them.
3. Anchor them in your body by noticing where you feel them. Where do they live?
4. You can also touch your forefinger and thumb together which helps to anchor them in your brain.
5. When you stretch the moment and encode it in your awareness, it will live within you long after the moment has passed.
6. Then you can call them back and revisit the experiences and the good feelings, drawing on those in times of need or when you want a boost.

You are literally exercising a particular part of your brain that houses your overall capacity for joy and happiness. We feel joy in our bodies because of the release of dopamine and serotonin, two types of neurotransmitters in the brain. Both chemicals are heavily associated with happiness; people with clinical depression often have lower levels of serotonin.

Although joy and happiness are natural emotions, they don't always happen naturally, which is why it can be helpful to practice.

- Is your happiness dependent on outside factors?
- Can you be content, even happy, when things aren't "going your way?"
- Do you notice any flickers of goodness right in the midst of dealing with challenges?

Jill Bolte Taylor, a remarkable neuroanatomist, observed her own stroke in her thirties while she was actually having it. She later documented that experience in *My Stroke of Insight*, speaking about the changes she has observed in her own brain, evidenced by her behavior before and after her stroke.

> "... the most fundamental traits of my right hemisphere personality are deep inner peace and loving compassion."

A Harvard-trained, self-driven, and accomplished scientist before her stroke, she delighted in noted changes after her stroke that engaged other areas of her brain, such as the creative side, never before as prevalent.

Calling herself a "brain enthusiast" she goes on to say, "I believe the more time we spend running our inner peace/compassion circuitry, the more peace/compassion we will project into the world and ultimately the more peace/compassion we will have on the planet."

Practice. Practice. Practice. Compassion. Peace. Happiness. Let's spread it across the world.

What you think matters. What you do matters. Your thoughts, beliefs, and actions are ripples on a pond moving outward and washing up upon the shore of the world around you. They seep into the ground and nourish creation in your outer life, too. You have the power to make life happen. This moment impacts others. Be more aware of your choices, moment by moment, so you might season the creation of what you desire.

> When you do things from your soul
> you feel a river moving in you, a joy.
>
> ~ Rumi

Gratitude

Do you approach your day from a glass is "half full" or "half empty" point of view? Do you habitually notice what is wrong or not working or do you count your blessings?

One of the best ways to treasure your moments is to focus, often, on what you are grateful for in your life. By noticing and calling out that goodness, you celebrate it. And, in a way, you perpetuate it by sharing that positivity when you acknowledge it with others—especially the good you see in them. Encourage and compliment people freely and honestly. You will be glad you did. Remember to encourage and compliment yourself, too.

A Daily Gratefest

A gratitude focus is not meant to be a denial of reality, one where we only look at what's blooming rosy. Rather by appreciating the gifts that are found in even the most challenging times, we stay present to the moment and its potential for good. Sometimes, from our point of reference, what looks unfavorable, even downright awful, may contain an advantage of some sort.

> An old Sufi story tells of a man whose son captures a beautiful, wild horse. All his neighbors exclaimed how fortunate he was. He replied simply, "We will see." One day the strong horse threw the son from his back. The son broke his leg and now, the neighbors proclaimed what a curse it had been for the son to ever find that horse. And the man said once again, "We will see." Soon after, soldiers came to the village and took away all the able-bodied young men, enlisting them to do battle, but the son with the broken leg was spared. Again, the neighbors observed how fortunate the man was for his son to be left with him. Once again, the man patiently said, "We will see."

>> This being human
>> is a guesthouse,
>> every morning a new arrival.
>> a joy, a depression, a meanness
>> some momentary awareness comes
>> as an unexpected visitor.
>>
>> Welcome and entertain them all!
>>
>> Even if they're a crowd of sorrows
>> who violently sweep your house empty of its furniture.
>> Still, treat each guest honorably.
>> He may be clearing you out
>> for some new delight.
>>
>> *~ Rumi, A Sufi Poet*

We never know how events ultimately will unfold. So, even in times of turmoil, an approach of gratitude can be useful. That lens brings meaning to the challenge and comfort to the pain. The practice releases the struggle and acknowledges it as having purpose.
By finding the good within the challenge, we can rejoice amidst life's suffering as well as its joys.

I recommend a gratefest before breakfast or before bed:

Make a list, write in a journal, or speak aloud what you are grateful for in your life. You literally create an atmosphere of appreciation, which builds on its own vibrational momentum, creating even more to be thankful for!

A joyful spirit is evidence of a grateful heart.

~ Maya Angelou

All of Life is Precious

I have encountered those who have said, "I have been on my spiritual path for three years now." Oh, my, NO! You have been on your path—the physical, mental, emotional, and spiritual path—since you were born. Whatever you have done and whatever you are doing is important. Everything is a part of your vast picture, a part of your personal story. Everything has significance. Whether you are accepting an award, discovering a new theory, breaking an athletic record, drying a child's tear, sitting in a chair reading this book, cooking a meal, planting a garden, or cleaning a toilet—you are on your path.

Life is precious. We are all headed somewhere in our lifetime. Our lives have meaning and purpose. Along the way, we are presented with many choices. Some are mundane, a part of our everyday ... and others are monumental, setting the tone and rhythm for years to come. There is no one right and perfect direction, but rather endless possibilities, a vast potential for your personal experience and individual expression. If life is a canvas, you hold the brush. And you get to choose the colors and the textures for your own masterpiece! It is your birthright to decide how you wish to shape your reality.

Even the most challenged person has choices. When he dives in and seizes the choices of his choosing, a pivotal shift occurs. No longer shipwrecked, grasping to a small piece of security as he floats along on the ever-changing tide without any control or direction, it is as if he has been given a paddle or an oar and can now row toward the shore. He may even acquire a sail or a motor and tool along at great speeds in the direction of his hopes and dreams.

There is value in all you do. Do you realize that? Do you live in that place of knowing everything matters? It is the way you approach your moments and the value you attach to them that colors your experiences. Being productive. Resting. Discovering something new. Battling an addiction. Disagreeing. Tormenting or anguishing over a deep wound. Finding solutions. Playing. Loving. All of it has meaning—it is living. And doing it your way rises to the opportunity of life.

> Be yourself. No one can ever tell you you're doing it wrong.
>
> ~ *James Lee Herlihy*

My Native American teachers taught me that there is a line of souls just waiting to incarnate into this earthly plane. The nuns at my Catholic School professed the same message. I have a feeling many traditions do. The meaning is clear; there is an understanding that life is precious. Regardless of your spiritual orientation, or whether you even have one, do you feel that way?

Do you know that this life, *your life*, is so very precious?

Even if you believe in other lifetimes, you will only have this lifetime once. That time is now. So, don't waste your precious time. Appreciate all your moments because when you connect them together, those moments shape you ... **and Turtle Wisdom reminds you that it's pretty incredible that you get to be you in this life. Out of all the possibilities, YOU are here right now.** You've got to love it!

To finish the moment,
to find the journey's end
in every step of the road,
to live the greatest number
of good hours,
is wisdom.

~ Ralph Waldo Emerson

No one else has
exactly what you have ...

... without you those pieces
would be lost.

7

I'm Stuck with Me!

OK. So, I must ask, do you ever feel "stuck" within your body, limited by the scope of your character—wanting more than what you, so far, get to be? Are there days when if you could, you would step aside, go in another direction, or even run away from yourself? In fact, some of us do, in one way or another, run from knowing ourselves, from truly knowing who and what we are and how we wish to express ourselves. But you cannot escape! No matter what—when you stop avoiding, moving away, or running—there you will be.

So, what can you do when you feel that way, when you feel victim to your own circumstance, and powerless to change it:

- Begin by standing in the presence of where you are, owning your personal ground, and being honest about what you see.
- Be true to yourself by claiming a welcoming space where you can be exactly who and what you are, without judgement (even if it doesn't look pretty).
- Then, honestly feel the feelings. Feel all your feelings even the uncomfortable or distasteful ones.

Among the most basic emotional needs we have is being allowed to experience and express our true feelings. We need to know that someone accepts, perhaps even understands those feelings, rather than trying to suppress or change them. We need to provide an atmosphere of safety for ourselves.

- It is from that place of acceptance that you can clearly assess where you are ... and where you would like to be. From that honest perspective, you can strategize how to move in your desired direction and who might help you in your evolution.
- Be true to yourself. Give yourself some slack as you are in the process of becoming, as you reveal more and more of your true self. Honor the process of evolving into the great potential that is You.

Becoming
Tossing and turning
In life it is that way
Move forward, set
sometimes a slow pace
Make choices, hear voices
which ones will you choose?
Decisions, revision
is changing your views
You recreate yourself everyday
Unbecoming, becoming, what you choose
There are no mistakes
there are no regrets
You just re-choose to be you
Finding yourself.

~ Author Unknown

And for those times when you feel captive in your own skin, a prisoner within your own life, I suggest working with the example of the snake, which sheds a layer of her skin to bring forth a new one. Turtles don't actually step out of and leave their entire shell, but adult turtles do shed shell pieces known as scutes as they grow.

Whether you shed pieces of yourself or an entire layer, you, too, can refine and recreate yourself. You can reshape your attitudes, beliefs, and expectations. Try on and play with your different "skins" as you see how the energy of them affects you and affects others around you. Try changing a habit or pattern of expression—if you are perpetually grouchy, try putting on a smile. With practice, it may become your natural way of being. If you talk incessantly, try being still to listen; observe what you learn in the silence of your stillness. Do something uncharacteristic: alter your outer expression or your way of being in the world. You might be surprised how different the world around you seems when you shift your way of relating to it.

Shed the old and make way for the new. Transform yourself into your next phase of becoming by consciously choosing to move in that desired direction. And if for some reason you don't like what develops, you can always peel another layer, make further changes, and continue refining yourself.

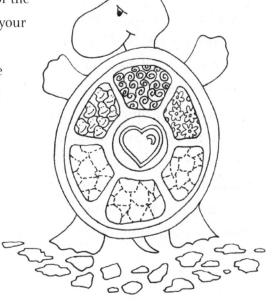

> Let's accept our humanity, with all its foibles and vulnerabilities, as well as its wisdom and power. There is perfection in your imperfections! You are who you are. Whoever you are has value. Look at yourself in the most open manner, so that you can get to honestly know yourself more fully and welcome that unique person with open arms. You are that magnificent masterpiece taking shape and form.

The Power of a Hug

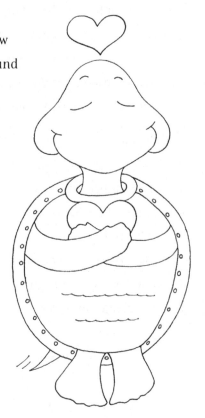

In doing yoga one day, I discovered how wonderful it was to wrap my arms around my upper torso and stretch—literally giving myself a hug. It's fun to see how far you can stretch, and it feels fabulous to be hugged, even by yourself. Try this. Do it first with one arm on top ... and then switch with the other arm on top. Pause in each position, taking time to sense how it feels physically and emotionally. No matter what's going on or how you're feeling, you can always nurture yourself by pausing and giving yourself a little hug!

When You Stand Alone

I suspect that most of us, by nature, are people oriented. Certainly, we are raised in our culture to care about what others think. We value being accepted and liked, and at least part of the time, we try to comply with what others request of us. So, it seems that it may take an effort to learn the skill of standing alone—to learn to be alone and to appreciate being alone. It has been said, "We come into this world alone and we leave it alone." Yet while we are here, we often crave companionship, outer validation, and love. What a powerful stance to learn to provide validation and love for ourselves. Then, anything else can be the whipped crème and a cherry on top!

When you are content with yourself, there can be a peace to being alone because there is less static from outer activity, enabling you to sculpt your environment in the best way for your safety and comfort. And you have the silence to hear your own blessed thoughts.

Confidence and Self-Esteem

How confident are you in who you are and in your ability to navigate through life? How would you rate your self-esteem? Would you say they are high or low or somewhere in between?

Self-confidence and self-esteem are related, but they are not interchangeable. When you possess valued characteristics or abilities and believe you can perform well in certain situations or certain roles, you typically develop confidence. When you are proficient, there is often a sense of having some positive control over your life and a consistently dependable confidence may ensue. But positive self-esteem does not naturally follow. It, too, needs to be cultivated.

Let's take a deeper look. Warning signs of low confidence may include:

- Feelings of self-doubt
- Passive or submissive behavior
- Difficulty trusting others
- Feeling inferior to others
- Overly sensitive to criticism
- Feeling unloved

> Confidence is your belief in yourself and your abilities, while self-esteem refers to whether (or not) you appreciate and value yourself. Self-esteem may be affected by those around you and how they react to you. Do they seem to value you? A person can be very confident in their abilities, but still have low self-esteem. Self-esteem is related to self-love. If you want to have good self-esteem, you must learn to love yourself.

Here are a few signs of low self-esteem. Notice if any of these seem familiar:

- Negative self-talk, harsh judgment, constantly criticizing and putting yourself down.
- Avoidance of social situations or feeling anxious and uncomfortable in social situations. May avoid eye contact, feeling unworthy of others' attention. Feel lonely, yet unable to reach out.
- Need for validation; may seek reassurance from others.
- Procrastination or lack of motivation.

- Difficulty making decisions, second-guessing yourself, and relying on others to make choices for you.
- Difficulty setting boundaries; often saying yes to things you don't want to do or allowing others to treat you poorly.
- Fear of failure; may avoid taking risks or trying new things because of the possibility of failing.
- Perfectionism: striving for perfection in everything you do, setting yourself up for disappointment and feeling like a failure if you fall short. Feeling like nothing is ever good enough. This one, unfortunately, is very common.
- A people pleaser; striving to feel good enough.
- Self-blame for things that are not your fault or taking on too much responsibility for negative events.
- Difficulty accepting compliments or positive feedback, feeling like you don't deserve it or that the person giving the compliment is just being nice. We've already looked at this one and considered how to change it.
- Comparison to others; feeling like you don't measure up or aren't good enough.
- Overall feeling of unworthiness and/or feeling unlovable.

Low self-esteem can have many root causes. Here are a few of them:

- Difficult childhood experiences such as abuse, neglect, constant criticism, or rejection can leave a lasting impact on a person's self-esteem.
- Cultural and societal pressures to conform to certain standards of beauty, success, or behavior can cause individuals to feel inadequate and lower their self-worth.

- Comparing oneself to others and feeling inferior can contribute to low self-esteem.
- Traumatic events such as accidents, illness, or personal loss
- Being in unhealthy or abusive relationships
- Mental health conditions such as depression, anxiety, and eating disorders
- Failure to achieve goals or meet expectations
- Difficulty in completing tasks and a lack of confidence in one's abilities
- A lack of recognition or positive feedback from others can cause people to feel undervalued and unappreciated.

Low self-esteem can affect every area of your life including personal relationships, social interactions, career, and overall mental well-being. It can also manifest as eating or other disorders, drug and alcohol abuse, and self-harm. If you recognize the signs or behaviors of low self-esteem, I urge you to seek support to address the underlying issues.

> Building self-confidence and self-esteem is critical for living a happy and fulfilling life. If you don't believe in yourself, life itself is a challenge. Even the smallest task can seem daunting. And a sense of happiness seems miles away.

I watched as this woman entered the store, coming in the exit door and walking in my direction with a strong purposeful gait, as if she were on a great mission. She quickly approached me and pointed to the stack of books to the right of me asked, "Are you the one who wrote that book?"

"Yes, I am," I replied as I watched her face soften. She told me her 15-year-old daughter had been meticulously planning the details of her suicide when her best friend gave her *Turtle Wisdom: Coming Home to Yourself*. The young girl told her mother it was why she didn't do it. The grateful mother came to my book signing to buy three copies: one for her daughter, one for herself, and one for the teen's therapist. It was a relief to hear the girl was getting help for what led to her wanting to take such a tragic step. If you or someone you love is on that dangerous precipice, please, reach out for professional help. Talk to someone. Tell them what is being considered. This is not the time to keep secrets.

Both confidence and self-esteem are inside jobs. Monitor your inside chatter to neutralize negative words and encourage positive ones. Find ways to acknowledge and appreciate your own value. And even if it doesn't seem completely real yet, encourage yourself to act more confidently, stretching into the experience of it.

Foster positive self-esteem by practicing loving yourself. If it is difficult for you to think about loving yourself, try this: when you think about someone or something you love, imagine drawing an energetic thread of that feeling—that love—and connecting it to yourself. Anchor it right to you! And then be aware, so you can recognize those moments when you feel a sincere sense of love for yourself and then, praise that feeling. Appreciating and loving yourself can be a learned behavior.

Confidence and self-esteem are a part of the core of who you are: they color all you experience and all you do in the world. Without a doubt, others may try to knock you down by projecting negative thoughts unto you. They may sometimes criticize you or convey a message of you not being good enough. You must attempt to combat those erroneous influences. Watch also for the feisty inner critic throwing self-defeating thoughts your way. In these situations, you can note the input without allowing it to take you down. Remember those comments can roll right off—like rain on the turtle's back.

Reach in and touch your worthiness, so you can fill your cup of confidence. Tell yourself how precious and deserving you are, even on the days you don't do your best. Believe in yourself and trust in your own abilities.

Greet life with a more positive outlook and a confidence that overflows. Draw on that resilient inner core and there will be no stopping you, because like the turtle, no matter what, you just keep moving on.

Do You Ever Ride the Superiority/Inferiority Wary-Go-Round?

> There is no private 'good'
> in God's neighborhood.
>
> ~ *Michael Beckwith*

Have you ever noticed another's faults or inadequacies with intense fascination? Or compared yourself so you could feel better, more accomplished, more evolved? When we feel our worthiness at another's expense, we play into the superiority/inferiority cycle.

We don't need to draw on some false sense of superiority at another person's expense. What is behind our critical thoughts? Typically, it is an underlying fear of others discovering our insecurities, our faults, our weaknesses. Therein lies the subtle panic of being seen, revealed for our imagined weakness, exposed for not being smart enough/capable enough/pretty enough/ strong enough/or _____ enough. Underlying a superiority stance is a deep dark layer of doubt. By comparing ourselves favorably to another, we somehow feel better, but it's fleeting; our comparisons ultimately add to that looming sense of inferiority.

The antidote is to realize that we are all works in progress. We are each valuable just as we are. What may appear as flaws can now be recognized as "under construction" while we enhance our personal character. We can envision and stretch toward the potential of the greater expression; the person we might be.

Shadows are illuminated with the light of our kindness and good intention. As we embrace a perspective of self-acceptance, we can see other people in a brighter light, too. Supporting each other offers a positive contribution to the overall human balance. Being patient with others perceived shortcomings—and understanding they are continuing to evolve—positively seasons the human condition, enhancing interconnection and strengthening our natural human kinship. This approach is a simple, yet truly profound life practice.

> Life never has to be overwhelming when you have someone that you can depend on, someone whose assessment you trust and whose opinion you value. Risking change is easier when you know that you have "you." Pack your turtle shell with confidence and keep moving! Your little mobile home with all you need goes with you ...

Perfectionist Perfect

What do you expect from yourself and others? Are you constantly imaging "if only" ... if only he would; if only I could; if only, you know, she really should ... When we project our imagined idea of perfection onto people and situations, we limit our ability to enjoy the richness of what is happening in those precious moments. We create a setup for failure because it can only look one specific way or else it's unacceptable. No one and nothing will ever be good enough. Most especially, ourselves.

Develop an awareness of when you are polluting the moment with limiting expectations. Stop yourself and notice what is before you—just as it is. If you can find one positive aspect about what's there, then, you have made a start. A guru once commented about another, "He feeds the plants with his out breath!" Now, that's stretching to find something good to say!

You know, even our "imperfections" *are perfect*, for in those shortcomings—mistakes we make, or failures we experience—we learn. We learn valuable information and insight that helps us to grow. So, allow yourself the space to just be. Your birthright *is* "the right to be." Begin with a sincere appreciation of where you are right now with the vision of how you are evolving toward your next greater-yet-to-be.

Life truly is precious. And you get to live it. So, live *your life* instead of missing it by living in the longing for something different. Know that all is ultimately perfect, every person and every moment precious.

> There is beauty in the onlyness of our snowflake selves—
> the unbeauty comes in not knowing it.
>
> ~ Rusty Berkus

The Process of Becoming

When you look at a baby, all fresh and new, do you ever think about what she can't do? Do you focus on the fact that she cannot walk or talk or build a sandcastle? Or do you simply view that baby in appreciation for all her potential ahead of her? It would be helpful if you could look at yourself in the same manner—recognizing the potential for becoming more of who you are and expressing more of your goodness, even your greatness. When you still have life ahead of you, it's never too late to be who you might have been. As long as there is life's breath within you, there is time. Seize the day.

And just as you wouldn't expect the baby to learn everything they have to learn without ever making a mistake, you need to muster the patience to be kind through your own process of discovery and learning, too.

> The great inventor and celebrated genius, Thomas Edison, taught us a lot about "failures." Although he did love to read, he did not do well in school so he was home-schooled. Edison was fired from his first two jobs for being "non-productive."
>
> He made 1,000 unsuccessful attempts at inventing the light bulb. When a reporter asked, "How did it feel to fail 1,000 times?" Edison replied, "I didn't fail 1,000 times. The light bulb was an invention with 1,000 steps."
>
> He said that many of life's failures were experienced by people who didn't realize how close they were to success when they gave up on their idea or their dream. A perfectionist would not try and fail 1,000 times. A perfectionist would give up in despair when the first few tries seemingly didn't work, thinking himself a failure.

> The most important thing, I think, is to fail
> at some point, so when you work your way back,
> you can say it wasn't all luck!
>
> ~ Barbara Walters

> Be courageous. I have seen many depressions in business.
> [We have] emerged from these stronger and more prosperous.
> Be brave as your fathers before you. Have faith. Go forward.
>
> ~ Thomas Edison

Rosie Rottencrotch

With her face just inches from mine she looked straight in my eye, pointing her finger at my nose, almost touching its base, and said, "You, Donna DeNomme, will never amount to anything." I blinked. She was the vice principal in charge of the girls at my high school and I was a defiant, acting-out teenager.

Still, in that moment, when I blinked, I knew it wasn't true.

Regardless of my physical reality, I believed that there was more to life ... and that someday I would experience it. I still had hope.

Okay, her name wasn't really "Rosie Rottencrotch," but that was honestly how we referred to her—because despite being a pretty young woman, she had a stern demeanor and was quick to judge, quick to hand out reprimands or punishments. Miss Rose never seemed fair to me; certainly not understanding or wanting to encourage us to become our best selves. As a teen, she was a harsh part of what I saw as those in charge.

But I have to say, years later, as a single mother—when I graduated first in my college class—it was her face that flashed in my mind's eye. I once again felt the defiance of my youth ... and I cut out the newspaper articles showing me receiving several awards and the highest of honors, stuffed them in an envelope, and mailed them to her.

"Don't you ever tell another kid that they won't amount to anything." my sticky note read.

Bright Reflection

A mirror practice can be used to develop self-acceptance. We can utilize the process introduced earlier in this book with the added addition of looking deeply into our own eyes. It's not necessarily easy to do! But it is something that gets easier with practice. Approach looking at yourself in the mirror with acceptance and curiosity. Who is this precious one before you? On your worst day, look at yourself in the mirror with kindness and compassion. Be patient with her; she needs your tolerance most of all.

- Compose a positive statement about yourself. You might think it in your mind or write it in your journal first if you need to practice it.
- Look at your reflection in the mirror.
- Now, speak your affirmative statement out loud with honesty and conviction.
- Repeat. Speak it out loud with honesty and conviction.

- Notice if you allow those words to penetrate inside of you. Do they reach your heart?
- Or do you block them, resisting their entry. Do your words bounce back off you? Do you let them drift away before they penetrate to your core?
- Monitor your reactions and strive to be more comfortable in accepting and believing warm sentiments. Practice your ability to sincerely receive compliments. Be willing to accept praise.
- Be grateful for the qualities you possess and the person that you are sharing with the world.

Jean Houston recounts the story that every morning anthropologist Margaret Mead would bellow in her largest, affirming voice, "Thank God, I'm Margaret Mead."

Go ahead, try it, "Thank God, I'm _____."
(And don't you dare say Margaret Mead!)

"Nothing Ventured, Nothing Gained"

> Be like the bird,
> who halting in his flight
> on limb too slight
> feels it give away beneath him
> yet sings, knowing he has wings.
>
> *~ Victor Hugo*

A long time ago a friend listened to me describe what was then a very limited lifestyle and heard me describing it as "safe and predictable." This friend looked at me shocked and horrified and remarked, "How boring! Nothing ventured, nothing gained." That statement was a catalyst for a two-year exploration that took me where I never dreamed of going. I received a scholarship to Cornell University and left the security of the small-town I had been living in to be in a city filled with people from all over the world. It was my awakening to a much larger community.

From then on, I adopted the same philosophy of "nothing ventured, nothing gained" and the adventures have continued. I have taken people to swim with the dolphins, led sacred ceremonies on remote, ancient Mayan ruins, taught Divine Feminine appreciation to teen girls, shared open conversation with incarcerated women, and written this book inspired by that philosophy.

In turn, I, too, have challenged many others tucked in their comfortable ruts to climb out and stretch further. It was as if one dear friend encouraging me to reach for more, dropped a pebble in that proverbial still pond, which continues to ripple onward today. Her comments altered my life, and in turn, touched others through me.

> So, what would you do differently if you adopted
> this "nothing ventured, nothing gained" approach?
> What is it you dream of doing?
> What is it you long to be?
> How might fear be holding you back? Or limiting you?
> Choose to be bold in your next steps.
> Claim expansion in your life.

There is a reason why you are in human form in this particular place at this specific time. Embrace your humanity; rise above the human condition by knowing that despite your imperfections or limitations, you are a perfect and brilliant work in progress. You have a gift to share that no other can give. You were created perfectly with all the means to bring forth that contribution from within you. Enhance and expand your outer expression based on your true inner core, following your own inner compass which will lead you to your best future. Allow yourself the consideration, the time, the space, and the nurturing to evolve into all that you can be. Be gentle with yourself and honor each and every part of your becoming. For every step has value, every stage merit.

> The journey in between
> what you once were
> and who you are now becoming
> is where the dance of life
> really takes place.
>
> ~ *Barbara DeAngelis*, Real Moments

Shapeshifting—
Powerful Personal Transformation

We are at a pivotal point in our human evolution. It is time to expand our ability to shape and reshape who we are, and to maturely sculpt our future from a place of conscious choice. We can no longer be at the mercy of what life gives us. We cannot allow ourselves to feel trapped within our own skin, prisoners to the human condition. Rather, we must be empowered to create the life we envision and manifest our dreams. We possess the potential for shifting into a dynamic way of being—if we can recognize our personal responsibility for how we are living and our ability to successfully effect change in our own life and beyond.

There is inherent goodness that seeks a path of expression through you. Explore the great unknown and live in a way which brings forth a planet that we have never seen, a reality we have only glimpsed, and a future bright with potential. If you want to experience what you have always experienced, then keep doing what you have been doing. If you can envision a grander scheme, then shapeshift!

> If you don't like who you are and where you are,
> don't worry about it because
> you're not stuck either with who you are
> or where you are.
> You can grow. You can change.
> You can be more than you are.
>
> *~ Zig Zigler*

Imagine your evolved life. See and claim your realized self.

You Get You ...
someone to believe in.

8

Difficult Days

*Sometimes I feel surrounded by a sea of negativity
that seeps through my muscles, deep into my bones,
triggering darkness within. Anger, confusion, fear, and chaos overtake
me, if for but a brief moment, and I am immersed in that overwhelming
darkness, until once again there is a glimmer of light.*

I wrote this in one of my moments of despair. For me, gratefully, these moments are fleeting; most days I embrace life with a positive attitude and an open heart, poised for the gifts and the challenges I may encounter. But we all have those difficult moments and we all have those difficult days.

For some, it's more complex and may color all else. There are those who struggle, unable to find a shred of happiness in their days. Like a heavy, low-hanging ominous cloud that follows them on their path, they are deeply discouraged, stuck in an ever-repeating unhealthy rut that bogs them down for even the simplest tasks. There may be a hopelessness they try to outrun in an attempt not to sink into the darkest pit of perpetual despair.

What I know is regardless of how complex or overwhelming your darkness is, regardless of how difficult the difficult days are, there is a way out. And the quickest way out is through! The fastest path beyond the darkness is first to acknowledge it and admit it is there. And because you honestly cannot outrun it, you must turn toward that darkness with curiosity and gentle compassion. Look it right in the face and see it for what it is. Feel the emotions that you are having (or blocking) and be open to what they can tell you. Our emotions can be guideposts. If we have the inclination to "read the signs," we can gain useful information as to how to move in and through what is causing them.

It was during my darkest times, coping with facing and healing long-carried wounding from childhood sexual and ritual abuse, that my inner guidance, my saving grace, said to me, "The quickest way out is through." They visually showed me the path—not an easy one, but one quite doable.

You cannot escape yourself, regardless of how hard you try. You are there, at your every turn, at every life experience. So, at some point, a choice must be made. Do you keep attempting to escape something that is inescapable? Or can you be brave enough to take a stand, gather the forces, and make your way in and through what needs to be confronted; so you may rise from where you are to journey toward where you really want to be.

If what you are dealing with seems too enormous for you to handle alone, reach out and ask for help. Sometimes this difficult step takes immense courage. Try. Push. Encourage yourself to trust a caring outsider who may see a different vantage point and be able to help you in even the worst of your situations. They can offer a place for you to safely share what you are going through and witness the changes you are attempting to make. Perhaps you have a good friend or family member who can be trusted to show up for you in this objective way. If not, don't settle for someone who may rewound you or harm you with neglect; reach out to a trained professional. Keep yourself safe.

> Trouble is bound to come,
> so cultivating the right attitude is crucial.
>
> ~ *Dalai Lama*

There is a worthwhile point of understanding even if it is covered in sticky muck that pulls you down like quicksand. Underneath all the murkiness is a place in the darkness that when illuminated reveals meaning and purpose to what you are experiencing. Perhaps, you'll even discover information that helps you determine your next chosen direction. Pushing through to find what's hidden below can truly harvest gifts. You may be inspired to make changes or encouraged to create a new way of being in your life. Get your feet dirty by tromping through this uninviting territory; get your hands dirty by sifting through the disgusting muck; uncover the gems hidden within.

> Something to consider: When you call it abuse, trauma, persistent pain, or repressed wounding—those are big, powerful words, describing big, powerful concepts.
> But when you call it "ick," you take it down a notch; it loses a part of its power. "Ick" is not so overwhelming.
> "Ick" is quite manageable.
>
> Everything that happens is a vehicle for your awakening—including the ick! Everything holds the potential for insight and understanding, for greater evolution of the self.

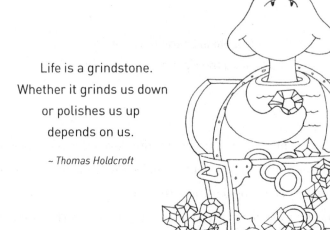

> Life is a grindstone.
> Whether it grinds us down
> or polishes us up
> depends on us.
>
> ~ Thomas Holdcroft

A Painful Place

Even though we might not like it, the purpose of life is not to avoid pain. In our quest for personal and human evolution, pain, at various points, is inevitable. We all experience pain on many levels. Of course, there is physical pain, mental, and emotional pain. And there are many painful nuances, too. There are implications in the conscious, as well as possibilities from the subconscious that may go bump in the night, waking us from an otherwise sound sleep. There are the emotional heebie-jeebies—things that are not defined, but you can feel them painfully there.

> Pain. We all have it in one form or another. It's what we do with it that counts. Do you wallow in your pain? Whine about it? Hold it up as a badge of accomplishment in front of the face of others? Pain is inevitable; suffering is optional.

You can try to minimize your pain whenever possible and certainly avoid perpetuating it. But accepting pain as a necessary part of life gives you the freedom to address your pain and move on. Life can be lighter and freer when you move through, rather than struggle with your pain.

There is a sacred path leading from pain and suffering to the meaning of our wounds. And wild success lies waiting on the other side.

Happiness is a choice and a skill to be developed.

> The sun shines no matter what is in front of it.
> ~ Author Unknown

I Still Feel "Not Good Enough"

What are the places, the roles, or the situations where you still feel "not good enough?" No matter how much work you do on yourself, there may still be times when you buck up against something you are not capable of accomplishing. When insecurities surface and hold you back or get in your way, there may be a blinding glare of self-worry or self-condemnation—not capable enough ... not rich enough ... not pretty enough ... not accomplishing enough ... creative enough ... not good enough. Operating under the assumption that "I don't deserve ... am not worthy of ... will never have or do _____." What is this self-defeating mind chatter about?

> My Native American teachers have shown me that it is for good reasons that people, by nature, are often insecure. All of creation has its strengths and weaknesses. Compared to the other animals, in many ways, we are wimps. We must

wear clothes to protect our bodies from the elements. Our vision is not as sharp as the hawk, nor can we navigate in the dark night like the bat. The mountain lion can sense movement at great distances and protect her territory. Ants, with their keen ability to cooperate, can move objects far heavier than their tiny bodies. For our size, our intelligence, and so-called dominion over the earth, we humans have a lot to be insecure about. At times, we may ponder what strengths we can develop to be more like our fellow earth mates.

The point is to get over it. Get over worrying about the fact that you are insecure and instead learn to deal with your insecurities when they surface.

- Notice your insecurities and feel the sting of recognizing your shortcomings.
- Then, examine your insecurities, evaluate them, and learn from them. Through the process, you can then obtain an understanding of what is relevant and what is not.
- Does this insecurity have validity? If so, what can I do to delve into ways that address this shortcoming?
- Or is it blown out of proportion somehow? Is my inner critic wreaking havoc again?

Learn to discern and sort what is meaningful from what is debilitating. Glean understanding. Recognize where the insecurity may have originated and what purpose it might have served. Honor the message that is there, without letting a sense of unworthiness rule your life. One by one, you pull the strands of understanding and transform them, until finally the cheerleaders are louder than the critics and you know and feel your worth. Like a fine wine or an aged cheese, you have carefully and lovingly nurtured yourself in seasoning over time, honoring the process. You have drawn forth wisdom and strengthened your core; you sincerely know your own worth. You recognize that you are worthy of all you may achieve or acquire in this life, and you savor the experience of life itself.

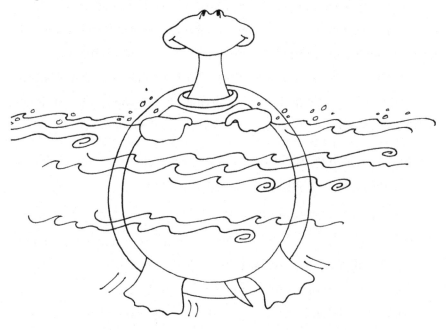

There are two ways of meeting difficulties.
You alter the difficulties, or you alter yourself to meet them.

~ Anonymous

Of course, we humans do not have dominion over the earth as some of us might sometimes think. One of the lessons we can learn from nature is the concept of competition vs cooperation. In some instances it may look like species are in competition, but if you look at the larger picture there is often an underlying cooperation there: the relationship of predator/prey keeps animals in a healthy balance without one species becoming too large and overtaxing the environment; organisms or diseases affect the trees which helps thin out the forest and prevent rapid spreading of forest fire; and forest fire itself is another of nature's balancing forces.

Draw forth wisdom by looking at how you view the natural world around you and the people who inhabit that world. Because you will experience a very different world and a very different life if you view everything around you as waiting to harm you in some way. Contrast that with believing that everything that crosses your path is ultimately there in support of your overall growth and development.

How does each perspective feel? One is poised for battling problems, the other pregnant and nesting with possibility.

Learn to tread lightly as you recognize your individual thread in the overall web of life and how tugging on your one thread impacts others. If you recognize that no matter how lonely you feel, you are not ever alone, but interconnected in that overarching web, you can imagine that all is unfolding in synchronicity for your good. Even that which doesn't look encouraging is still part of the overall beneficial whole. There are no mistakes in the essence of evolutionary creation—all have a "right to be," including and especially, you!

I am worthy, simply because I am.

~ Dr. Robin Smith

> It is by no mistake that
> you are a part of creation.
> YOU have a right to be.
>
> ~ *Turtle Wisdom as taught through
> a Native American lineage*

Following are helpful perspectives to deal with difficult days:

Unravel the Messy Ball

As we move through life's challenges and changes, it is often as if we are sorting a knotted, entangled ball of twine—complex and scratchy. Rarely does anyone have one simple problem or one simple shift. Often many things occur simultaneously. In addition, there are subtle nuances within each piece, creating influential threads that are all enmeshed in a complicated entanglement.

My most effective approach is to grab hold of a thread—any thread—and work it out. Sometimes it may not be the core issue, but rather the one that is the easiest to move. As we address various threads (issues) and separate them from the entanglement of the ball, the congestion becomes more open, less enmeshed. It is much easier to manage and eventually may completely unravel, allowing us to wind up the ball in a proper way.

The "string" is now available to reorganize in a more suitable way or can even be used to create something new.

I have found that this visual image enables us to release the sense of struggle and instead try to unravel it all. It inspires us to be patient with the process of difficult times and to release any need for a quick fix. This understanding allows us to take the time to get to the roots of our difficulty, so we can bring forth a deeper level of healing and more permanent solutions.

> I've already mentioned that when I attended Cornell University studying Human Development and Family Studies, I was a single mother of a bright, five-year-old. He was (and is) remarkable. One morning Todd was up on a kitchen chair with a large, colorful apron laced around his chest, washing a few dishes that were in the sink. It was one of his favorite pastimes and one I was pleased to encourage. Todd watched as I dashed this way and that trying to get ready for our busy day. I needed to walk him to school with lunch in tow, finish a paper to turn in that afternoon, and make the long trek up the hill to get myself to my first class.
>
> After watching me take a few hurried laps around the kitchen, Todd said, "Mom, focus on one thing at a time. Do that. And when you're done, go on to something else." Wow! "Out of the mouths of babes," as they say. I looked at him in that oversized apron and burst out laughing, as much at myself and my running in circles that morning. Todd reminded me to slow down and focus moment-by-moment. That slower, more relaxed, and less demanding perspective can effectively serve us when we need to unravel our troubles.

Reaction or Creation

When we are under great pressure or stress from challenging situations, it is quite common to be reactive. At times, we may take it personally as if someone or life itself has it out for us. Or we may fall into old, not-so-great patterns of coping with what is before us. This is an area we can choose to rework so we might find better methods for meeting and processing turmoil.

- Consider how you show up in situations that are typical for you.
- Are you reactive? Or do you act from a place of deep consideration and conscious choice? Or a combination of the two?
- Monitor yourself to see if it feels like a personal attack.
- Or if you feel like a victim to someone or something.
- Create a circle of conscious awareness as you look in front of you, behind you, all around you, and within you, gathering all that information.
- And then ...
- Try not to take it personally but instead rise to the challenge.
- Choose how to move forward by repatterning old behaviors to be in alignment with your "now" and your personal integrity. Stand on your own character.

Choice is the ultimate super-power!
And *you* have it! We all do.

So, ultimately, you get to choose how you react. There may be that initial knee-jerk type of reaction, but you get to repattern and shift it; and, over time, new pathways will be created which will become the norm.

Think of that ball of string once again, only this time let's create a tapestry with our threads. You get to choose what and how. Draw from the old; you'll see what you want to keep moving forward and you can weave those various parts back in. They are perfect just as they are—and strong cords woven together won't break.

On the other hand, you may choose to "snip, snip" old ties of those no-longer-needed pieces and let them fall aside. You can shed layers and layers of what's no longer useful or supportive. Other parts and pieces may need to be colored or refined. You might also want to hold the space for the resolution of an unsettled piece; sometimes we must deconstruct before reconstructing to create something new.

As you refine yourself by stripping away what isn't authentically "you," you reveal your best version. When the bulk of your creation is drawn from the inside out because you weave from your own personal integrity—your true colors—you will never go wrong. From your efforts, you see a stunning tapestry made from all the shades and textures of the various parts of you. To deny any piece of your life's creation would do yourself a disservice. It would be like leaving a significant strand out of your finely woven tapestry. What do you value about yourself? What aspects don't you value? Imagine what it might be to embrace them all ... and then shape and reshape your greatest creation into the masterpiece it deserves to be.

Following are simple techniques to help deal with difficult days:

Bitchin' Buddies

Years ago, I developed an effective strategy for handling difficult times. When someone is upset, angry, frustrated, or even perplexed, it often helps just to vent their thoughts and emotions. I invite people to simply "bitch" non-stop for fifteen minutes, to get it all out, without concern for how they sound. No editing or censoring. Just spill the whole mess, stink and all. After a time of just being with the content and how it feels, after the wildest whirlwind has been released, we can begin to break it down and separate it into sections. We can look at:

- What is significant and what is inconsequential.
- What is reactive and what is an honest take-away.
- What is true assessment and what is being seen through an old lens of distorted perception.
- What is not worth continuing to carry in its present form but might need to be let go or transformed into something more useful.
- When done properly this technique can alleviate the inner pressure of pent-up thoughts and emotions yet be a way to let go and move on.

I suggest you have a bitchin' buddy. Someone you can talk with freely, who allows you the space to acknowledge your "poor me" day. Someone who understands that right now, in the middle of the whirlwind, it is difficult to be you. Your buddy holds a basic belief that when you vent this way, what you say is not necessarily exactly what you mean. You are just blowing off steam and it is the turmoil that may need this outlet, clearing the way for what you really mean and how you ultimately feel. A bitchin' buddy can be invaluable in this process because she is safe. She is just there to listen, not to judge or try to fix you or any of the mess you are sharing with her.

One important point of this approach is that at the end of your allotted time, when you have gone through your story and expressed your emotions around that occurrence, there reaches a point that you must stop. The goal is to let it out, leave it on the floor in front of you (or more appropriately, behind you), and then turn from it and walk away. You let it go ... Do not reel it back in and begin again. Do not lament, bemoan your circumstance, or wail from the depths of your being for days on end (unless, of course, the situation truly warrants it). Don't revisit it later like a bad habit. Do not make this bitchin' buddy stance a familiar groove that you play over and over again, wallowing in it. Use it, lose it, and move on.

> Remember the steam kettle.
> Though up to its neck in hot water,
> it continues to sing.
>
> ~ Anonymous

Forgiveness

Let's nurture our garden of inner peace.
Cultivate contentment and allow it to bear the fruits of
love and forgiveness, growing in each and every moment.

~ Robin Maynard

Do you hold onto resentments about your past? Do you still feel anger or bitterness from injustices done to you? It has been said that holding this kind of negativity is like drinking poison and waiting for the other guy to die—its toxicity destroys you.

What negativity do you need to empty? Are there memories that haunt you, attitudes or emotions that have outlived their time of productivity? When we first experience a disappointment or a painful interaction, our emotional reaction is a part of the natural processing and healing. But it *is* a process and as such there should come a time when we move from the place of reaction into the time of release ... and we rightfully turn our attention to other things.

During the course of your life, you learn that the person who wasn't supposed to let you down, does. Your heart may be broken more than once, maybe too many times to count. It hurts. But if you honestly assess what has passed, you have to admit that you've hurt others too. You let someone down or left them behind in your dust. You had a falling out with someone in your family or maybe even fought with your best friend. You blamed a new love for things your old lover did!

Who do you need to forgive? Can you also forgive yourself? Letting go of old resentments, hurt, anger, and bitterness frees up a lot of internal space. This is a creative space! How could you redesign it to better reflect your unique goodness? Let go of that dark, dank toxic sludge and bring forth more of you. Fill that spot with the truest expression of your beautiful core essence and the gifts and talents you possess. Because when all is said and done, you may want to reclaim lost opportunities, judge people less, and be more tolerant. You may want to let go of "either/or" polarized thinking and instead see the nuances of greys in the shadows. You may want to savor the promise of what's around you and open your heart once again, even if you've been hurt because your interest, your attention, and your love are meant to be shared.

> Forgiveness is giving up the hope that you can change the past.
>
> ~ *Anonymous*

Oops! Cancel! Cancel!

Each thought, every word, every action has a unique vibration that impacts our experiences. There are times when you think, say, or do something that is not aligned with your genuine intention. There may be a tendency to just let it slip by, hoping no one else notices, but be careful of what you put out there.

When you are out of sync and express from an off-kilter place that is unlike your true self, you don't have to ignore it, hoping it will go away. You can neutralize your faux pas. "That was stupid," you say to yourself under your breath when you make a mistake. Oh, my. Cancel! Cancel!

Give yourself another chance to express it more appropriately, "Wow, look at that ... I won't do that the same way again!" Words are powerful. Even spoken to yourself when no one else can hear you, unproductive criticism can erode confidence and self-esteem. Be kind when speaking to yourself. And refine your patterns of expression to be more clearly in alignment with what you wish to say.

- Recognize the power of your words. Notice what words you use and be aware of their true meaning.
- Be mindful of your actual honest intention.
- Find ways to weed non-supportive comments out of your vocabulary.
- Say what you mean and mean what you say and if, in some cases, that is not very nice, well, so be it. At least you know that you consciously chose to put that vibration into the flow of things.
- When you mistakenly say or do something that doesn't match your truest intention, catch it, and neutralize it with something more aligned.
- Oops! Cancel! Cancel!
- Then, speak what you really want to say.

This canceling technique is not meant as an excuse for you to say and do horrible things, thinking that you can cancel them afterwards. You are responsible for what escapes your mouth and the way in which you interact with others. You are accountable for what you put out into the world, and yet, it is energetically sound to recognize that our mistakes are sometimes made unintentionally. And this is a beneficial way to clean them up.

> Cancel! Cancel! = a quality control effort for conscious, energetically-aligned living.

Our lives are often filled with trials and adjustments according to what we learn in route. This technique is more than a word play—it is an attitudinal shift. Its message strongly conveys, "Hey, wait a minute *that* is not what I really intended. What I really meant was _____." It is an effective method to refine your self-expression.

Some people have found it particularly impactful to use an invisible eraser to literally swipe the air in front of them, erasing the words they have just spoken. "Cancel! Cancel!" They visualize the words completely wiped from the atmosphere right in front of their eyes. Regardless of whether or not you physically erase, remember the power of canceling and neutralizing words that are not in alignment with what you genuinely intend. Mean what you say and say what you mean, so you can create your desires through your very own potent words.

Refining Old Thoughts/Beliefs

> Your beliefs become your thoughts,
> your thoughts become your words,
> your words become your actions,
> your actions become your habits,
> your habits become your values,
> your values become your destiny.
>
> ~ Mahatma Gandhi

Our thoughts and beliefs are foundational to every other part of our personal expression. So, we must monitor our thoughts and explore our beliefs to assure they are in alignment with our core values for what we wish to bring into the world. At times we may need to adjust our beliefs or refine our thoughts to have a truer self-expression.

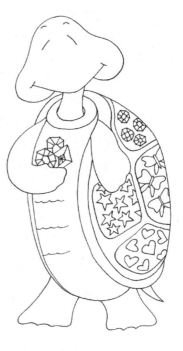

When striving to reach toward a higher level of expression, many of us have found affirmative statements to be helpful. You can use words or phrases which are meaningful to you personally—those power-packed words that go right to the heart of the matter, perhaps even sending chill bumps up and down your spine. Use these effective, affirmative words to refine or enhance your thoughts, foster a new belief, or encourage a new behavior. Potent words empower you to grow beyond where you are right now and help you stretch toward where you have yet to be, to help you embrace your greater-yet-to-be potential.

If you desire a new improved financial flow, focus on positive thoughts that shape a healthy financial future, "I make sound financial decisions," "I manage my money wisely," "I spend within my chosen budget," and "I have an abundant source of financial prosperity."

> Kristi and I met weekly for a couple of years to co-coach, providing each other worthwhile support. We comforted each other through disappointments, encouraged our bravery, and held the vision for our dreams. When Kristi

decided to focus on attracting financial abundance, I was taken back by the strength and conviction of her words when she affirmed, "My financial good comes to me from all directions, in all ways right now. I open my arms wide to receive my financial abundance. I don't care if it literally falls from the sky. I open to receive my financial prosperity now!" And she spread her arms wide, outstretched above her, as if to literally catch the money she wanted to receive.

Well, I observed her receiving several surprises in the form of financial gifts over the following weeks—like unexpected refunds or credits on her credit card statements, or the time she had to purchase something and unexpectedly found the price had just dropped moments before because of a timely sale. Someone even mailed her a sizable check, without any communication, to pay an old debt she had completely forgotten having loaned.

One Sunday, Kristi and her husband were on the way to church when they noticed what looked like money floating in the air over the highway. They pulled over. Once they could retrieve one of the pieces of paper, they saw that it was a $100 bill! And there were many more floating up and down, this way and that in the currents of the passing cars. Well, they collected the bills, one by one, which took them quite a long time—it was a major interstate highway. Luckily it was Sunday morning and there wasn't as much traffic as there would usually be. Even though it was tedious and treacherous work, they did so as a team grabbing anything that came close and periodically dashing out when there was a lull in the wave of passing vehicles.

Here's the remarkable thing. No one else stopped. Perhaps they didn't believe that real money could actually be floating around on I-25. It took them several hours but when they were done, they had retrieved over $10,000.

Being upstanding citizens, they drove to the nearest police station and reported it. They turned the money in ... and waited. Then something truly miraculous happened. After ninety days, they received a phone call to come pick it up. No one had claimed it! The police said it was most likely "a drug deal gone bad" and some money went out a window. With no one or nothing to connect it to, it belonged to those who found it.

My friend's words reverberated in my mind, "I don't care if it literally falls from the sky. I open to receive financial prosperity now!" Wow!

Okay. So, I have to admit it. I've tried the same affirmation without the same results. But it did open my financial flow in a way that made sense to me. Belief is a powerful force; and honestly, I'm not sure I believe it can fall from the sky the same way Kristi did.

Ultimately, this mindset shift is an inside job. We can only receive equal to our ability to open to receive. Which is why it is essential to work on our own thoughts, attitudes, and beliefs.

One technique I learned years ago that really helps get past the part of the brain that doubts or resists change is to say, "In the past this was true, but what I know now is ...." For example, "In the past, I had some difficulties managing money, but I now make healthy choices in how I spend my paycheck."

> Reframe and repattern:
> "In the past _____ was true,
> what I now know is _____."

As you guide yourself to develop in a desired direction, there may be times when your thoughts or actions may still mirror your "old" beliefs. By noticing your thoughts, and the words you use to describe your thoughts, you have a golden opportunity to shape and reshape your words to reflect the new evolved you. By changing what you think and say about yourself, it reinforces your evolved self and propels you even further in your new chosen direction. It provides momentum and the power to continue moving forward in a positive way. When you shine the radiant light of your attention on your words and actions, refining them when necessary, you provide a brilliant sun to help them grow in a way which is sturdy and resilient.

> One of my closest friends called me one day with excitement overflowing in her voice, "I found it! It's amazing. It's the size I've been looking for with perfect sound quality ... and on top of that, it's on sale. Today is the last day. What do you think, should I buy it?"
>
> I could hear the salesman behind her saying, "You're not gonna get a deal like this one again. You're crazy if you don't get it."
>
> "STEP AWAY from the TV," I spoke into the receiver with a slightly raised, and intentionally firm voice.
>
> "But ... but ..."

"You are going in the wrong direction. ... This is not the time ... BACK AWAY from the TV," I repeated, "Just let it go."

Dianne was working on restructuring on a financial level and this expenditure was not in her best interest. Which was why, of course, she called me. Months later, when she was in a better place financially, she purchased an even better television with all the bells and whistles.

Now is a fertile time for you to refine your thoughts and beliefs. What no longer serves you or the life you wish to create? How can you alter those thoughts and words, or repattern your behaviors to come more in alignment with your truest intentions? Don't wait another day to choose authentically meaningful words and compelling, dynamic actions that vibrate out and draw in the experiences you wish to create.

> Yesterday is ashes,
> tomorrow wood.
> Only today does the
> fire burn brightly.
>
> ~ Eskimo Proverb

Keep Your Sense of Humor

Every oak tree stated out as a couple of nuts
that decided to stand their ground

~ Henry David Thoreau

Whenever possible, keep your sense of humor. Life brings many fascinating coincidences, curious happenings, and outright cosmic jokes! If you feel as if you are laughing with life instead of being the brunt of the joke, your experiences will be lighter and freer.

Blessed are you who can laugh at yourself
for you will never cease to be amused.

~ An Old Saying

I've Been Lost and Now I'm Found

Have you ever lost something and then later discovered that you still had it, usually in the last place you'd think to look for it? Or perhaps exactly where you did look for it a hundred times, but for some reason you didn't see it right there in that very spot! Do you remember what it felt like to lose something precious and then rediscover it? Relief. And Joyful, right? There are precious times when we rediscover a lost part of ourselves: it may have been there all along but inaccessible, or it could have been buried under wounding or strife, or it may be a younger part of yourself that comes back around from a new perspective.

I have a middle-aged student who recently said to me, "I feel like I am back where I was when I was twenty. I am sensitive to the world. I am open and acutely aware of what is around me."

"What is different this time?" I inquired.

"My acceptance of it," she said.

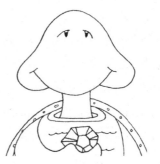

> Our greatness lies
> not so much in being able
> to remake the world ...
> as in being able
> to remake ourselves.
>
> ~ Mohandas K. Gandhi

Mohandas K. Gandhi (1869-1948) was a lawyer, a politician, and a powerful activist in the struggle for social justice and for India's independence from British rule. He is internationally known and honored for his doctrine of nonviolent protest (satyagraha) to achieve political and social progress. Instead of fighting back, Gandhi stood in the face of great danger, was jailed for civil disobedience, and fasted for long periods of time in protest of the injustices he saw. His efforts led to many advances in this regard. He was loved by many, then and now.

Gandhi is best known as saying, "Be the change that you wish to see in the world." I find it fascinating that his activism gained him the title Mahatma, meaning "great soul." What a great man and "Mahatma," what a great honor.

Just like Mahatma Gandhi's non-violent protest, there may be times when it seems like you are sitting still; it might look like nothing is happening to move forward in your life. But no matter what, you are progressing. Even when you can't see it, there are energies gathering and micro-movements being initiated. Which is why we focus on our attitudes, beliefs, thoughts, words, and actions, right? It is how we affect change.

When you find yourself returning to a place where you've been before, or when you see an old trait or behavior resurfacing, notice what is different this time around. Can you find meaning or insight in the changes? Whether you would consider it a positive or negative behavior, you may have progressed on the upward spiral of understanding and have a more refined awareness about this aspect of your being. Draw that realization forward so you might deepen within it even further.

Embracing Change

Life may be uncomfortable or even painful, when undergoing even the simplest of changes. For those who resist change, the most desirable alteration can still be threatening. I try not to use the word, "comfortable," when describing a possibility. We might feel quite uncomfortable when navigating a chosen and valuable shift in our inner or outer reality. We might not be ready to go in a different direction even when we're unhappy with where we are presently. We might have to stretch and grow to accommodate what's needed to meet a particular challenge. Our resistance to change may limit us. But if we take the "comfortable" or "ready" expectations out of the equation, then, like the turtle, we can take one step and then another and then another. We can find the inspiration and the strength to move forward.

> If there is no wind, row.
>
> ~ *Latin Proverb*

An inspiring speaker, Dr. Fred Vogt, used to say, "Yea, though you walk through the valley of the shadow of darkness ... *don't build the condo here!*" His compelling message is that we will have difficult days and challenging times, but we don't have to get stuck there. We don't need to wallow in the torment of it or perpetuate its occurrence. No matter what you are confronted with, keep moving ... keep moving.

Even the slightest movement can make a helpful difference. When you feel stuck or stagnant, aim to create a positive motion that catapults you forward. Recognize your abilities, your skills, your gifts, and all those who support you; draw those building blocks in and construct your house on that foundation. With that solid groundwork, you can then trust in yourself as you keep moving in your desired direction.

Like birth, your growth may be painful, but a new expanded life awaits you. So, comfortable or not, if you see your next chosen move, go ahead and take it. Ready or not, here you come.

> Minimize what depletes you
> and maximize what supports you.
>
> ~ *Turtle Wisdom*

If you want to awaken all of humanity, then awaken all parts of yourself. If you want to eliminate all suffering of the world, then eliminate all parts that are dark and negative. Truly, the gift you can give is that of your own self-transformation.

~Lao Tsu

The call of our time is to transform old dark sludge into new potential.

~ Donna DeNomme, 8 Keys to Wholeness

During my "Writing Immersion," I meet with a handful of people who come to my meditation garden. We circle as a group to delve into something inspirational or contemplative, and then we scatter to our own special spot in the garden to write, uninterrupted for a nice chunk of time. We repeat this focus several times throughout the day. I've found this pattern optimal for helping people tap into those deeper, vaster spaces ... and to bring forth the gold. A grief counselor and gifted writer, Patrick Fitzgerald, was part of one of these groups recently and after a solitary time of writing while perched on an unusually tall chair with the ability to peek over the back fence and gaze off across the field to the Rocky Mountain foothills just to the west of me, he shared, "I spent most of my time thinking about what came through and spilled onto my page," Patrick said, "May I read it to you?" "Yes, please do."

In a solemn voice Patrick spoke slowly, enunciating every word. His words had great strength as he said, "Love is both mountain and water. And how do I *be* that?"

There was an immediate resonance to his words and their impact reverberated around our small circle. Some spoke about what it meant to them; others sat in awe with genuine appreciation. The longer I sat with it, the more I realized it was like a Zen Koan. I could contemplate this statement over and over for a month and probably still get new insights. And love *is* both like a mountain, sturdy and dependable, offering a challenge to climb to new heights *and* water—flowing, refreshing, and ever-changing. Love isn't something you learn and master in a short time. Love evolves.

As I was completing this chapter, it struck me. "Difficult Days" are both mountain and water, too. We have the challenge of climbing steep terrain, traversing scary heights, and being supported by sturdy and dependable ground beneath us. At the same time, our difficulties are fluid and moving, changing shape and form. Water is often associated with emotions, including the dark murky depths we must plunge into in times of turmoil. Yes, Patrick, your little Zen Koan can really serve us here. And so, I invite you to contemplate what meaning you can glean (today and tomorrow) as you sit with this idea.

> Difficult Days are both mountain and water.
> How do I accept and rise with that understanding?
>
> *~ Turtle Wisdom*

The Human Spirit
is never broken; never lost ...

Reach inside and
touch your Core Essence.

9

The Alchemy of Your Troubles

> Alchemy: Any seemingly magical power
> or process of transmuting.
>
> ~ American Heritage Dictionary

What is the Point?

There is a point. I promise you. Every experience, every challenge has one. We may not always realize it or learn from it, but it is there. A pivotal shift occurs when we tap the precious potential within that deeper understanding by opening to the underlying message of our personal turmoil.

> A single event can awaken within us a stranger
> totally unknown to us. To live is to be slowly born.
>
> ~ Antoine de Saint-Exupery

Life has difficulties and challenges. Each of us has our own version of them. If we don't take it personally when hardships come our way, we can look at the bigger picture, the broader understanding. Yes, I realize that these hardships are happening to us so I guess, in a way, it is "personal" and at times, it may even seem like someone or life itself has it out for us. But the truth is, ultimately, it is happening for us. Our challenges are the spice of life, drawing forth the richer flavors of who we are in the face of them; it is part of the territory of self-discovery. It is often through these trying times that we discover a new way, grow closer to those we love, or learn more about our own inner character. If we encounter challenges with a faith in our ability to move through them and an openness to the valuable meaning they may hold, we'll have the inner push necessary to navigate through them more easily.

Let's envision that everything that happens to us is conspiring for our greatest growth. Then we can view all of it as a part of our unique story. And if everything is contributing to that story, there is no need to despair even in our darkest hour. If someone is doing something to us, for whatever reason, we can still hold the intention that there is an unknown purpose and we can rise to the situation in a way that is constructive, instead of being defeated by it. We won't let it taint our view of life or our ability to move through our challenges successfully. And we let each situation and each individual stand on their own merit, instead of extrapolating to the whole.

> It's madness to hate all roses because you got scratched with one thorn, to give up all dreams because one of them didn't come true, to give up all attempts because one of them failed. It's folly to condemn all your friends because one has betrayed you, to no longer believe in love just because someone was unfaithful or didn't love you back, to throw away all your chances to be happy because something went wrong. There will always

> be another opportunity, another friend, another love,
> a new strength. For every end, there is always a new
> beginning.... And now here is my secret, a very simple
> secret: It is only with the heart that one can see
> rightly; what is essential is invisible to the eye.
>
> ~ *Antoine de Saint-Exupéry*, The Little Prince

See the silver lining in the dark clouds, the rainbow after the pouring rain. Just as we need the clouds and the rain to nourish the grass and trees, eventually we notice the inherent value in even our most difficult days. It's also helpful to make a comparison between your difficulties and the other parts of your life. What do those comparisons point out? What insight do you find held within those contrasts? Remember you cannot see the stars until they shine in the darkness of the night sky. What do you see because it's been highlighted by the darkness of your own hardships?

Greet the world in an open and receptive manner despite what transpires. You can do so if you are genuinely secure within yourself regardless of any chaos created by these trials and tribulations. In all the ups and downs, you remain the hero or heroine of your own wisdom story, in every single part of it.

Be real and acknowledge what is; be sincere in your reaction to it. As you realize the value of these difficult life experiences, there's no need to shrink from them or cower in fear, nor do you respond enraged with overwhelming anger. You meet them full on as you move right through the difficulty. You rest in the comfort that you can do this—whatever "this" may be.

> When everything seems to be going against you,
> remember that the airplane takes off
> against the wind, not with it.
>
> -Henry Ford

Where you are right now and who you are at this very moment is absolutely, without a doubt, uniquely precious. No matter what may be happening in your life and regardless of any perceived shortcomings, there is nothing about you that is broken. You do not need to be fixed. There is a part of you which forever remains unscathed, intact, authentically you. Sometimes you must reach down very deep to find it again. Healing comes through bringing forth the part of you which is always well.

> Know that how you show up and work within adversity is what matters most. It is the character you bring to the hardship that ultimately helps shape you. And that character remains long after the challenge has passed; it is the legacy you leave behind, the imprint you impress on life's memory.

> There is an amazing
> resilience within the human spirit.
> This understanding brings
> acceptance and strength.
>
> ~ Turtle Wisdom

Trauma Dramas

Did you ever see someone hooked on the energetic high of discord and trauma? There is an intensity that's created when battling with others or dealing with crisis that can bring forth a great adrenaline rush that conveys, "I am ALIVE!" Some folks become vigilant in their guard, just waiting for the next injustice to fall, so they can rise with a vengeance and strike back. For some, these patterns were created in childhood, out of necessity, because they weren't safe and needed to remain acutely aware for sheer survival. For others, something may have happened later in life, causing them to develop this hyper-vigilance. If this sounds familiar, ask yourself is this hyper focus necessary (or healthy) now? How does it serve you? How does it hold you back? A continual "on-guard" stance can be taxing on your body and soul.

If your honest assessment reveals that this approach no longer serves you, then what might you change? This could be a multi-layered approach with behavior modifications to change your reactive patterns, as well as putting practices in place to help you feel safer. If you ask for help with your changes, that simple act of reaching out says that there are those who are "for" not "against" you. Be brave. Be persistent. These old patterns can be reprogrammed; you'll feel so much freer when they are. I promise. I know from having lived through it.

Oh! And fire yourself from the karma police! No longer will you be responsible for sorting out the world's wrong-doings, person-by-person. You are not the judge and the jury. Know that for all the times you have felt wronged, there have been others when you, too, in some way, have been the wrongdoer. Go from victim to victor. Let people be responsible for their actions and allow life itself to be responsible for their consequences.

And don't sweat the small stuff. Let the little things roll off your back. Your turtle shell is curved for this purpose. Learn to appreciate the richness of life and your high will come from the goodness all around you. Life, not turmoil will "charge" you!

True Traumas

There are most certainly traumatic times. You lose a job, a relationship ends, someone you love passes away. Some of us endure great hardships —physically beaten, raped, or worse. All of us sustain wounds in this lifetime; it isn't a contest, every one of them counts. Regardless of how big or small you consider your challenges, you matter. Your pain matters. We all face these trials and tribulations as a part of the human experience, so cultivating a productive attitude is key.

Even though some difficulties are heart-wrenching, dauntingly painful ones, it is truly amazing what people can do. It's comforting during these times of hardship, heartache, and woe to remember humans are remarkably resilient with innate healing abilities beyond description. We can heal from the most horrendous experiences. You can heal, too, no matter what. For those times when you feel literally on your back, stuck rocking back and forth with your feet waving in the air, remember Turtle Wisdom. If just one part of your foot can find your grounding on the earth beneath you, you can flip yourself over and begin moving again ... .

> Learn the alchemy true human beings know.
> The moment you accept what troubles you've been given;
> the door will open.
>
> *~ Rumi*

Gratefully, it is often during these journeys through adversity that we find our greatest gifts. The point is found in meeting and healing what is presented to you, surviving and then thriving beyond it. Through many years of listing to client's stories, I've come to believe that we draw to ourselves the experiences we need in order to develop into the person we were meant to be. These experiences may be challenging, even traumatic; sometimes "bad" things happen. But just as I've witnessed with my clients, I wouldn't be the person I am without the harshness of my childhood wounding. It has shaped who I am and the work I pursue. It was my initiation into my life's destiny. And although I might not have consciously chosen it, I can absolutely see the value in it. I believe the same is true for your wounding, your challenges, and the worst of what you've been confronted with—you are who you are, not in spite of it, but at least partially, because of it.

Alchemy Breeds Success

> You can't go back
> and change the beginning,
> but you can start where you are
> and change the ending.
>
> *~ C.S. Lewis*

Have you weathered an incredible storm, met an overwhelming life challenge, or forged uncharted waters only to come out the other side with increased confidence, enhanced life skills, and a great sense of accomplishment? I am not saying the experience was easy. In fact, it may have been deeply hurtful ... but when everything was said and done, the outcome had positive repercussions. In fact, they may have been downright inspirational!

Often it is through life's woundings that we are shaped into a greater way of being. As a piece of steel is tempered in the fire, we, too, transform through the heat of difficulties into a more refined "us." A terrible blow might spurt us in a new direction altering our life choices. Or our own pain may bring forth compassion and understanding for others.

> No one moves through life unscathed;
> in some way or another we are all the walking wounded.

When we consider the alchemy of our troubles, it's helpful to focus not only on the story of what happened, but what came forth as we went through those times—the strength we mustered to greet them, the new lessons and choice points we encountered, and ultimately, how we rose above what came our way.

- It is what you do with your wounds that creates the mark.
- Do you wallow in them? Become stuck in a place of hurt and despair?

- Do you repeat patterns? Or play over and over the same destructive cycles?
- Or do you shift, rising to a new way of being, adapting, learning, growing?
- The final point is not the wounding. It is only one part of what is ultimately a productive cycle.

- Where can you go from here?
- How do you continue? How do you heal?
- How do you eventually come to terms with your wounding? The growth is found in your healing.

When I was moving through the rugged terrain of my most difficult healing, my inner guidance inspired me with this hopeful understanding. It was the beacon that led the way to freedom.

> **The point is not the wounding:**
> **the point is found in the healing.**
>
> *~ Turtle Wisdom*

Wendy Cohen is the loving mother of a vibrant college student, Lacey Miller. Lacey was pulled over by a man posing as a police officer who kidnapped and murdered her. Although indescribably grief stricken, Wendy spoke openly from a place of compassion for the murderer's family, despite what he had done. She recognized that his family wasn't to blame.

Wendy showed such a centered conviction as she shared that Lacey's life was not defined by this one tragic event, but worth far more. Wendy's grief fired a powerful transformation as through her efforts, legislation was passed regulating the sale of the blue and red flashing lights used by police officers. From the tragedy of Lacey's death came efforts to prevent this loss from ever happening to another family.

As a teacher of conscious energy studies for over thirty years, I've seen many students drawn to healing practices because of a physical imbalance they've had or one they've been challenged with in supporting a family member. As a adjunct to traditional medical practices, individuals find value in studying alternative modalities. Some of those students have gone on to pursue advanced training, which has enabled them to open practices and assist others. Their personal challenge was an initiation into a greater calling. We must honor the catalyst that moves us onto new healing paths.

> Within me is Infinite Power, before me is Endless Possibility, around me is Boundless Opportunity ... Why should I fear?
>
> ~ Anonymous

- What unclaimed strengths do you carry inside your little turtle shell?
- What is your capacity for growth and evolution?
- If you can pull these aspects out and develop them by other

means, you may avoid the strife that otherwise might be necessary to coax them out.
- Look within the nooks and crannies of your "shell" and imagine all that you can be. There are gems hidden within you.

> There is no place of
> absolute security. In life, there
> are risks, there are difficulties. Shift
> from "Life is a struggle" to a lens of
> curiosity "Isn't that fascinating?"
> Treat life as a daring adventure,
> for truly, it is!
>
> ~ Turtle Wisdom

Round & Round We Go!

> Keep a green tree in your heart
> and perhaps the singing bird will come.
>
> ~ Chinese Proverb

When undergoing challenges, you encounter one perspective, then another and another; and sometimes end up back at your original vantage point, now with a different understanding. Your awareness of what is happening and the lessons you glean often grow in a circular, upward spiral. You may get stalled in an experiential groove which you play out again and again until you see another perspective or learn enough to catapult you to the next upward groove. To get that upward boost you must see the point (or points) of what you're going through—otherwise you stay stuck in what has been commonly called "Control

Dramas." Have you noticed patterns you repeatedly experience, never seeming to resolve or change? Some of us date or marry the same person in different bodies! This is a prime example of missing the ultimate point and getting repeated opportunities to catch it.

If we recognize this process as a natural, healthy, and even necessary cycle—that understanding then frees us from the frustration of thinking that somehow we are hopelessly stuck in a rut with no escape. Or that our fate in life is to suffer.

Patience and Persistence

> In the confrontation between the river and the rock,
> the river always wins ... not through strength but by perseverance.
>
> ~ *Unknown (two people claim it)*

We all know the story of the turtle and the hare. In the race, the rabbit sprints ahead only to tire and stop to rest. As he sleeps, the persistent, slow-moving turtle makes his way past, down the road, and crosses the finish line.

From this children's story, we see one of the messages of Turtle Wisdom. No matter how challenging or tumultuous life seems, just keep moving through those situations that present themselves. Keep going. Keep plugging away. As long as there is movement and growth, you are, like the turtle, heading in the right direction.

If we are alive, there is progress, even if you can't see it. The wisdom of the turtle is to keep moving, keep moving, keep moving. Little by little, change will occur and then you can look back with gratitude at what you have accomplished. Eventually you will see another landscape. From one point of view in your experience you may be unaware or unconscious of another viewpoint, not seeing what's just ahead. Once you visit the situation from various perspectives, you will see they all have merit, even the difficult ones. You can find meaning in each aspect as you develop a fuller understanding. Like baking a cake, the individual ingredients do not taste good, but when you put them all together, yummy!

Onward and Upward

Eventually you may see that your upward spiral is emerging. Even if it is a slight shift, when you come back around, you are clearly in a different place than before, a higher ground so to speak. You have learned new ways of dealing with that challenge or new ways of manifesting that achievement. You are moving onward and upward.

From this perspective, it may be easier to recognize and acknowledge everything you've encountered as a part of your process, seeing the meaning and purpose in all of it. That understanding makes it easier to see the potential in even the most trying of situations.

> **Release any need to look at your life through the eyes of the wounded one. Instead, create through the eyes of the healer.**
>
> ~ Donna DeNomme

> Affirm:
> Everything I do
> is perfect
> for my growth.
>
> ~ *Turtle Wisdom*

Where you are right now and who you are at this very moment is absolutely unique and precious. So, hold the vision of your upward spiral and know there is deeper personal growth happening no matter what it looks like on the surface. Recognize your experiences contribute to your highest evolution and how you show up and work with adversity is what matters most in those times. Handle what's in front of you, deal with what you can from your current perspective; glean the lessons of right now. And with the inspiration of the turtle, just keep moving. Put one foot in front of the other in your desired direction. Be diligent as you find the courage to move ahead; don't give up even when it gets tough. Keep the faith—and believe that your efforts will reap benefits. Observe where you started and how far you've come and use that awareness to encourage yourself onward and upward. The character you bring to these times is what helps shape you. Your core self is what remains long after the challenge has passed ... it is the imprint you leave behind on life's memory.

If we are facing the right direction,
all we have to do is keep walking.

~ Buddhist Proverb

As a child, I tumbled and twirled,
danced, walked on my hands,
swung upside down from iron railings,
did headstands, handstands, cartwheels ...
I missed so many years of the rhythms of my body ...
How could I have been absent for so long
from my own true self?

No time now for regret.
Only time to pay attention
to bring my awareness to the pleasure
of being the Prodigal Daughter
returned to my own loving arms ...
come home to my own body.

~ *Pamela J. Free*

PART III

10

Your Body, Your Temple

*Though we travel the world over to find the beautiful,
we must carry it with us or we find it not.*

~ Ralph Waldo Emerson

So, what about the little mobile home you tote around with you? At this point I have already invited you to consciously connect with the earth beneath you and the body you inhabit.

How does your outer shell serve you? It houses what is inside— your personality, your character, and your spiritual essence. It is the first layer of what protects you from the outside elements, the physical, mental, emotional, and energetic. Your body is not who you are, but surely it is an essential part of you. Your physical wellbeing is important to your survival.

How a person identifies with and cares for their outer shell reveals the truth of how she feels about herself.

- Do you take care of your body?
- Do you keep your physical container in good health, appreciating it for the role it plays, rewarding it with good food, exercise, and rest?

- Do you adorn your outer form, celebrating it as your personal expression?
- Do you enjoy the sensual experiences of the world around you, awakening fully to the ways in which your physical form interacts with and interprets the world around you?

For years I facilitated spiritual retreats to Mexico and one trip included a visit to a strikingly beautiful wildlife preserve. On this extraordinary day, there was an unusual richness of color. The sky was a vivid, clear blue with small, white, puffy clouds.

Our boat skimmed along the shiny water, a deep red from the mangrove trees, pushing its way through lush green jungle. The trees were draped with huge fibrous webs, glistening in the sun. As the jungle opened to release us from the narrow trail we had been navigating into a larger, open expanse, we heard a low gurgling off in the distance. Just beyond our reach was a distinctive hum unlike anything I had ever heard before—it was as if a hundred Buddhist monks were deep throat chanting in prayer, "Nnnnerrrrrrr. Nnnnerrrrrrr. Nnnnerrrrrr. Nnnnerrrrrr." Up ahead was a vibrant orange pink which grew deeper and brighter as we approached. For the first time ever, I delightfully greeted a magnificent flock of elegant flamingos mingling amongst themselves. What an incredible sight!

- Consider going on a sensory date
- Choose a place alive with activity: an auction, a craft fair, the circus, a concert, or the zoo.
- Notice all the colors, shapes, smells, and sounds as your experience the nuances of your day with the richness of all your senses.
- Feel your surroundings acutely.
- Be grateful for the physical body you inhabit and the physical world you have to explore. Enjoy the gifts this life brings!

Have already explored how you feel about your body and forged a greater alliance with it? How we relate to our body is quite individual. An eighty-pound anorexic can look in the mirror and see a much wider reflection. A physical feature which has haunted us since childhood may seem dominant and pronounced, looming as a shadow blocking our light, while to others it may be hardly noticeable.

In her empowering classic, *Healing Secrets of the Ages*, Catherine Ponder recounts the story of Myrtle Fillmore who had complex physical problems. Her body was wracked with pain and disease. This woman began a dramatic healing process simply by looking in the mirror each day and praising what she found good about her physical appearance. At first this was quite difficult, nearly impossible. There was a lot she didn't like and not much she could call "good." But as she made this technique a daily practice, her list of physical likes grew ... and as she praised her body, it responded by becoming stronger, healthier, and more outwardly beautiful. It blossomed under her tender attention.

We are in our bodies for a reason. Just like the turtle, you cannot escape your shell except to pass out of this world. So why not stand your ground, look yourself in the eye, and praise the physical vessel which supports you in such a direct manner. You will feel more present inside yourself. You will live and move from a more positive vantage point. You can still make improvements to your body in some way, if you wish, but begin with an acceptance about your physical body right now, just as you are. Then, if you look through that positive perspective, any changes can also be seen and appreciated. Even aging can happen gracefully.

Fully claim your body ... right now, just as it is:

- Make a promise to care for it properly.
- Consider what foods are best for you and adjust your diet accordingly. Feed your body with good fuel to energize your days and allow you to sleep peacefully at night.
- Think about exercise and discern what would be supportive for you. Choose something fun, so you'll be motivated to do it.
- Make good, healthy choices to support your physical self.
- How could you pamper your body? Some days a simple facial or foot soak can make all the difference.
- Nurture harmony with your physical self. Give it loving attention for the essential role it serves.

- Schedule in self-care. Get a massage. Go for a swim. Take a walk. Sit under a tree. Wrap your arms around yourself and give yourself a big hug.

Self-Care is Non-Negotiable

My friend takes nurturing self-care to a whole new level. If "self-care" was a competition sport, she would most certainly score a gold medal. Im-press-ive!

> She carefully creates a dedicated space each morning. Delicately spreading out her yoga mat, small weights handy on each side, she places an intentional (ever-changing) altar as a focal point at the head of her mat. Dianne puts on soft music and lights a non-scented candle. On any given day, a vision board (or two) might be propped up within view. She also prepares a healthy snack of a juice or blended smoothie, fruit in a bowl, or an energy bar cut into little squares; anything that is visually enticing and yummy to be savored mid-way through her morning ritual.
>
> Then, she begins.
>
> With a gentle bow, she bends down on her mat into a devotional pose, pressing her forehead into her mat and breathing slowly, in and out, in and out, slowing down her day from the onset.
>
> Moving into a seated position with her legs stretched out in front of her, she gently starts to brush her skin with a soft, dry brush. This centuries-old health practice is known for

its cleansing benefits as you exfoliate old skin cells making way for the new. She slowly brushes each leg and then each arm, tending them with loving care. After the brushing, she applies a favorite moisturizer, nourishing the newly exposed skin. She lingers on her feet, pushing on vital pressure points to stimulate organs. After taking her time with one foot and then the next, she moves to her hands massaging and attending to the pressure points there, too.

Simple, yet meaningful stretches follow, nudging the body to awaken further: seated forward fold, side stretches, downward dog, and warrior. She consciously and intentionally directs the energy created through her centering movements toward her altar space where she either has a saint or a person in need, recently her nephew in boot camp for the army. Ending on her back, she picks up the weights and does some arm exercises and crunches and leg rotations to build core strength. She alters what's done from day-to-day, listening to what her body needs. That fluidity, in itself, is a spiritual practice.

Then she slows further.... Snacks a bit on what's in her bowl or glass, writes in her journal. Pulls some inspirational cards and contemplates their meaning. Listens to her inner guidance and records the messages. Dianne onsiders options she's been presented with ... and opens the portal to possibilities.

Wow! **My friend calls this special time "non-negotiable."** As a deeply spiritual person and a successful businesswoman, she knows the value of self-care. And she has reaped the benefits. One morning inspiration alerted her to the fact that she was going in the wrong direction—and she swiftly altered her game plan. Another brought a desire to make a large purchase and within a week's time, she had manifested the ways and the means to do so. Other days, she finds a gentle peace and an evenness not evoked by anything previously. This morning ritual has literally changed her life. She guards this time with all get out. Don't try to reach her during "Samadhi." She won't answer the phone; it's silenced. Or to be more precise, it has meditation music steaming through it!

When I traveled recently, I observed someone in direct contrast to this ease-into-the-day approach. My sister hits the floor running in the morning and goes at full speed until she lays her head down at night. She is the epitome of a Type-A personality.

> "Hey, sister, come out on the boat with us and watch the sunset," I say.
>
> "I can't. I have too much to do."
>
> "Let's sit on the porch swing and chat."
>
> "I. Don't. Sit."
>
> Ishk! Life is too short not to be enjoyed.

I don't spend an hour or two immersed in restful and meditative pose like my friend. As a writer, I often find my way to the keyboard, capturing my early morning thoughts. But I do slow down and stretch precious moments of contemplation, insight, and joy throughout my day. And I've always had the tendency to stop and smell the roses, be immersed in gorgeous sunrises, soak in beautiful sunsets, and watch moments of curiosity and delight all around me. I truly savor life. And I am the better for it.

> How can you refine the way you care for yourself?
> **No matter where you put it in your day,**
> **find time for yourself. Find time for self-care.**
> Structure it in your schedule so it works best for you.
> You don't necessarily need to place yourself first as the
> top priority of your day—but you must be somewhere
> on your to-do list. What would serve you best?
> And how can you make that happen?

Simple pleasures are a basic need. They enrich your humanity and feed your soul. Be sure to recognize your body as the precious temple it is—this outer shell houses your unique personality and character; it holds steady your essential core self; and in this way, it is sacred. Treat it with respect and kindness, nurturing and care.

Right now, in your mind's eye see a picture of your body and imagine at the very top of your head a space of receptivity, a place that is open to "light." Your crown is the seat of the superconscious,

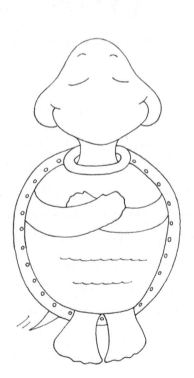

which can access inspiration, knowledge, enlightened understanding, and unexpressed potential. The crown of your head is a splendid gateway.

There are energy centers within you with a divine nature that is vital, active, and alive. It is what enables your body to function without your moment-by-moment attention to heartbeat, breath, and digestion. There is also a powerful innate ability within you to heal; *your body knows how to heal.* You can deliberately activate your healing capacity by inviting the divine intelligence within you to flow to areas of need. Just as you are minding your mind for what it is thinking, tap in and access how your body is feeling. Listen when it asks for your support; respond to its needs and wants. And when there are physical imbalances, call forth the body's innate healing ability to work in conjunction with what you are doing on a physical level. Send positive, uplifting, and comforting thoughts to your body, as you praise it for the healing process it is pursuing. Feel tender healing energy flow to the area of need, and watch as it moves downward into your toes and into the earth mother beneath you.

> You don't need to force healing to happen, you simply invite universal healing energy to go where it is needed with peaceful, gentle acceptance. Believe that your body is a safe space and a healthy container to carry you though life. Let that awareness seep into every cell, every muscle, every bone, and every organ.

Fall more in love
with your life
every day.

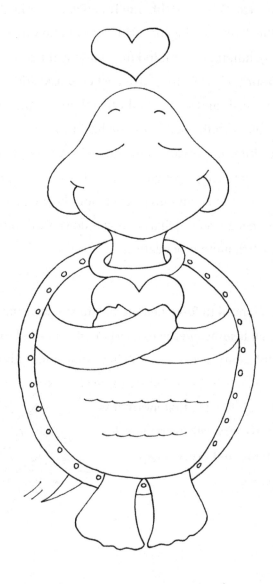

11

Exposing your Soft Belly

*I urge you, amid the differences present to the eye and mind,
to reach out and create the bond that will protect us all.
We are meant to be here together.*

~ *William Chase*

One sweet aspect of the human experience is our ability to share with each other in a way which is genuine and clear, presenting ourselves in a manner that fosters an honest connection with family and friends. If we take those precious personal connections and hold them close, they can help us cope with an ever-changing, unpredictable world. Long-lasting relationships create an outer stability, something to lean on in times of challenge.

If you want to cultivate sincere connections, you must strive for your interactions to reflect your authentic self. Someone cannot truly know you unless you show them "you." Are you willing to let down your guard, to be open and vulnerable? Whoever you are and whatever you have to contribute, there are others who can benefit from your gifts. Can you reach inside and share from your heart of hearts? Do your relationships resource the depth of your soul?

In the challenging aftermath of the tragedy of September 11, 2001, one positive ripple was the heartfelt caring demonstrated by so many in such a rich variety of ways. Whether it was helping the victims in some direct manner of service or holding a candlelight vigil for healing and strength, communities have rarely been so present with one another. In those moments of outrageous grief, we huddled together, trusted one another, and grew closer because of our shared trauma.

We ventured through another unknown territory of the greatest magnitude with the unexpected outbreak of the coronavirus world pandemic. We have never dealt with such a national and global health emergency in our lifetime. Neighbors helping neighbors was the very best part of this unsettling crisis. People stretched into new and creative ways of connection even when we were "sheltering in place." How can we foster that same unity without having to sustain another global tragedy?

Turtle Wisdom encourages you to call on your authentic core and your heart, as they are centered within you. Your core self is naturally grounded through its innate connection with the earth beneath you. If you tap into that earth connection, you can access your interconnection with everyone and everything, your connection with all of creation. When you offer your authentic self through actions that align your head with your heart, then it becomes much easier to find the courage to expose your "soft belly" to those you are developing relationships with—as you show them what is true, and sometimes quite vulnerable within you. When you are vulnerable in sharing your authentic self and the truth of your being, you are stretching beyond the protection of your snug little shell. Genuine connection often requires great trust.

For balance, there are also times when you may want to pull in and retreat within yourself; to shelter from the outside chatter of the world and focus on the guidance of your own core self and your own inner knowing. In other words, you "come home to yourself," you create and then nurture that warm and welcoming hearth of safety within you.

Of course, you can't move forward until you peek out of that shell and stretch out into the greater world again. Still, a turtle has a moment-by-moment choice of when and how far to stick her neck out, even though she won't get anywhere unless she does.

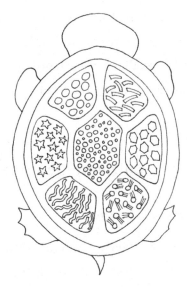

> The only way to have is to give;
> the only way to keep is to share.
>
> ~ George Booth

> When pure sincerity forms within,
> it is outwardly realized
> in other people's hearts.
>
> ~ Lao-Tzu

Will the Real You, Step Forward Please

> To be yourself in a world that
> is constantly trying to make you
> something else is the greatest accomplishment.
>
> ~ Ralph Waldo Emerson

You can create a more spacious home in the outer world by aligning your outer expression with your truest inner self and attracting toward you those who resonate with that expression. That camaraderie will provide secure places to retreat when needed, like another proverbial communal shell to shield you.

Give yourself permission to be yourself and in doing so accept that not everyone may like you. And in turn, give yourself permission to not like everyone else either. I have a friend who says, "those who are yours will know your face." She is referring to the distinct recognition that happens when we meet someone for the first time and there is an uncanny knowing that we are coming back together with a long-lost friend. It's as if we already know each other on an intimate soul level.

Cultivate Genuine, Authentic Connections

Eyes of the Soul

Observe how you interact with others. Do you look in their eyes? Do you open to those you encounter through the soft welcome of your gaze? The greatest gift we can give someone is our undivided attention and researchers tell us that 90% of our sense receptors are in our eyes. So, when you meet me and intently focus as you look at me—you see me looking at you, looking at me!

I am not suggesting that you stare at people, locked in on them with an awkwardly intense glare, but rather that you allow your beautiful inner essence to shine freely through your eyes. After all, there is a reason your eyes have been called "the windows of the soul."

> My friend Carl Studna, a world-renowned photographer, has the rare gift of being able to highlight the beauty in everyone he captures on film. He truly sees that unique life-spark within and coaxes it forward until it cannot be contained. It is expressed outwardly in the most delightful way resulting in stunning photos.

Carl has photographed celebrities for decades. I was honored to experience his photographic skill first-hand several times. Remarkable! As someone who doesn't necessarily enjoy being photographed, Carl makes it fun and easy. And almost every shot was a masterpiece. How does he do it? Well, it has to do with the eyes ... and he draws your authentic self out through them for those soulful photographs.

You can check out Carl's work in *Click: Choosing Love One Frame at a Time*. He talks about "opening to the inner and the outer light" in a way that chooses love over fear.

Power of Touch

Touch is also important. A gentle touch can bridge differences through an extended hand that offers a shared connection.

I want to acknowledge that there is a healthy balance here, too. Sometimes people can be overly touchy in a way that creates discomfort rather than appreciation. What about those close talkers who stand within your private space blowing their words in your face? There is an energetically acceptable balance of being present, but not encroaching into another person's natural boundaries.

Words Are Powerful / Thoughts Are, Too

Be mindful of how you speak to those around you. It's golden to know when to speak and when to keep silent especially when speaking up for yourself. Harsh or kind words can often come back to you in the reflection of another's words and actions. What do you wish to convey? What do you wish to place into action? What is the message or impression you'd like to put out into the world?

We've already explored the impact of "saying what you mean, and meaning what you say." In considering your intimate connection with others, you can also commit to minding your mind! Yes, "minding"—tending to it as if it were a small child in your care. Watching it closely, listening to its chatter, monitoring the thoughts as they go this way and that ... and measuring them next to the yardstick of your authentic intention. For if your mind is carrying on in a direction you'd rather not promote, realize you can shape and reshape it through conscious thought and purposeful action. You can choose the attitudes and beliefs that feed your thoughts every day. And if your thoughts are misbehaving, you can help repattern them by positively reinforcing the ones you hope to cultivate. Greater awareness encourages balance, alignment, and sometimes an energetic upgrade to uplevel your mindset.

Don't Let Others Define You

You have truly arrived when you can place yourself figuratively naked in front of others with no risk of having their reactions define you. You can choose to expose parts of yourself, including your soft belly, and others can comment or react, without their input devastating you. Their responses cannot erode the sanctity of your core self—your secure inner safety remains constant. Untouchable. Dependable. Your confidence in this core self pervades your experience. You can listen to others' reactions, weigh the information, and utilize it according to its pertinent worth. It may, in fact, help shape your evolving self, but it does not concretely mold you for your creative direction comes from the inside out, as you emerge more and more into the person you are meant to be.

Once you have developed your relationship with your core personality in such a way, it provides priceless inner security. You can risk being vulnerable in your interpersonal relations. Regardless of the situations or the people that you encounter, you can always rely on that inner resource for strength and guidance. Even though this core resides in your center, it radiates into all parts of your being. You can imagine that it also extends into a part of your "turtle shell," for it shields you in a strong, protective way from the outside world. You can depend on the safety of your core self.

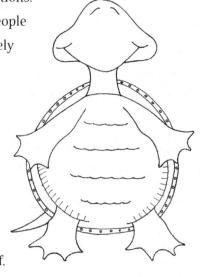

Free to Be

We invade each other's personal space by projecting our ideas of what we imagine or desire to be true about another person. Preconceived judgements squelch the possibility of genuine sharing. They stunt our potential connection as they inhibit our scope of interaction. Our misperceptions are tethers that limit our range of interaction and bind us in unhealthy ways; they tie us up in relationship knots.

Target these tendrils of subtle control that often permeate relationships:

- To release them, first identify and recognize their true nature.
- These ties convey our experiences and desires, pulling on others to comply with our wishes.

- We do this through our body language, our words, and the mental and emotional energy we exude.
- Our attempt at control stifles the opportunity for sincere connection.

It is such a heavy burden trying to energetically manipulate people. Even if we are subtly pushing our agenda, it can be exhausting. Let go of that useless task and you'll be amazed at how much relief you feel and how much energy you gain. Instead of focusing your attention on fixing and managing others, you can tackle your very own renovation project as you define and redefine yourself.

Embark on a welcoming path of true connection. Approach people with a genuine curiosity about what they might have to offer, so they have the freedom to share with you authentically.

It is through those open eyes that you truly *see* them.

It is only with the heart that one can see rightly;
what is essential is invisible to the eye.

~ Antoine De Saint Exupery

As you release the limiting interpersonal struggle for control that attempts to fit people into the nooks of your desires for them, what emerges is a more genuine and open interaction. When you respond to people and situations based on what is sincerely being expressed, a spaciousness is created, allowing for a true connection to blossom. People can be more honest with their words and actions and they tend to be much happier in a receptive environment. You can also rightly claim the same personal freedom for yourself. What may seem initially like a small difference can have a dramatic impact. Release your preconceived idea of how relationships should look and appreciate each one for the unique essence it brings.

> When you see that everyone you meet and everything that happens to you brings you lessons that are important for you to learn, you become grateful for everyone and everything.
>
> ~ *Gary Zukov*, Soul Stories

The Silver Platter

If you need to deal with strong points of differences which cause ongoing struggle in key relationships, I recommend a technique I developed for helping people let go of their side of the struggle. Like the child's game, "tug-of-war," you may feel swayed this way and that as you pull on your end and the other person tugs on theirs at the same time. What do you actually have control over? Only your end of the rope! When one person changes her attitude, her behavior, or her reactions, dramatic shifts can occur.

One empathetic approach is to come to terms with those differences by accepting the reality of both sides of the issue, recognizing that your perspective isn't the only one. You release the grip on your end to allow more space, no longer trying to force your point or attempting to sway the other in your direction. That doesn't necessarily mean there is an agreement or resolution; when there is no hope of an agreement, you simply release your tight hold on your end of the rope.

In your mind's eye, imagine doing what's necessary to virtually let it go. See yourself moving through this simple yet profound process:

- Take those qualities, personality traits, or life choices belonging to another, which you do not agree with or approve of, and let them go by placing them on an ornate silver platter.
- Picture the silver platter in as much detail as possible. Perhaps it looks like one you own or have seen before; perhaps it is one created purely within your imagination.
- Visually see yourself arranging the traits or behaviors on this beautiful, shiny platter in a way that is meaningful to you.
- Now offer the platter up. You can imagine reaching up and putting it on a shelf. Or you can visualize turning it over to your Spiritual Source.
- Either way, you let go of any responsibility for the other person's behavior or trait. You recognize whatever you have placed here as being a part of his/her choice, development, or growth. It is not yours to deal with, assess, or judge. You, in this moment, realize it simply "is" and it is outside of your control. So, you place it on this imaginary silver platter and let it go.

- When we do an internal process like this, we often see that it not only causes a shift within us, but furthermore, may impact outside physical realities as well. It's astonishing how an internal visualization can shift our outer circumstance. As we let go of the energetic entanglement, that release ripples forth to create anew. I have seen relationships plagued by discord remarkably changed with this simple process.

> I want to be clear that the work of the silver platter process occurs within you. Yet, the effects can often be seen and felt way beyond yourself in circumstances in your outer experience.

- You can also place aspects of yourself on the silver platter. Perhaps qualities or behaviors that for right now you don't wish to pursue, but instead choose to place aside for the moment, such as an instance of anger you don't yet fully understand but wish not to be consumed by any longer.
- You place it aside, not to avoid it, but to take a breather and gather energy and resources to understand and cope with it. You choose not to live in a place immersed in anger right now, but instead put it on the shelf or turn it over until you are ready to take it down and explore its true meaning.

This technique is not appropriate for every situation, nor is it suggested as a continual way to deal with interpersonal difficulties. Certainly, there are times when direct dialogue is called for, when each person can speak and be listened to, and perhaps reach an understanding and resolution.

> Utilizing the silver platter technique is one way to foster acceptance of another's differences (even when we don't like them), enabling us to build that relationship without the constant rub of ongoing irritation. It is quite helpful for those areas which are not really ours to change anyway.

For example, if you want your brother to interact with you in a certain way and yet, for many years, he has not done that, chances are his way of relating is different than how you long for him to be. Releasing him to his own rightful expression can be freeing, not only for him, but also for you. Relate to him as he is and open the door to a sincere relationship—whatever that looks like. Recognize the value in what transpires, rather than trying to force it to comply with your predetermined picture. If your needs are not being fulfilled by this relationship, give yourself permission to search out other ways to have them met. In this way, you no longer keep pursuing something where it just isn't available.

What I find fascinating is that time and time again when people release others from any obligation to fit into a preconceived mold of what they "should be," often they show up in exactly the way the person so desperately wanted. By letting go of their side of the tug-of-war, it releases ongoing struggle, frees wasted energy, and enables the other person to show up in their own authentic way.

> When we cut the
> chords of our expectations,
> it shifts our interpersonal dynamics.
> As we remove confining gates
> of limitations, we expand the
> scope of what might be.
> We let it unfold naturally.
>
> ~ Turtle Wisdom

My mother is a caring, nurturing person who spent much time with us baking, doing crafts, and teaching me how to read long before I went to school. She also was oblivious to the horrors of my childhood and not present to comfort or save me. For a long time, I unconsciously resented that. Then, I consciously resented that! When I shared my story with her, I didn't feel she showed up, initially, in the way I needed or wanted her to be there for my wounded inner child, or for me.

After some time of soul searching and years of healing, I realized that I wanted her to fit into my idea of what mothering looked like, my idea of what I thought I wanted. She is an individual with her own life path, her own needs, her own reactions, and her own perspective. It's just not right to expect her to morph into what I desire. It's a healthy part of our relationship development to go through that type of separation ... and acceptance. Letting her go to be her own person naturally shifted my behavior. I was no longer angry or resentful toward her. Those emotions had somewhat affected our relationship for years and now that pressure was released, allowing for a freer connection. I also recognized that I had unfulfilled needs and found that when I opened to accept what I needed from others, the right people were magically drawn to me. Gradually my wounds healed, and I became stronger and happier.

Right before Christmas when one of my most "mothering" friendships was undergoing a shift and fizzling out, I found myself very, very sad, overwhelmingly so. In a moment when I was unexpectedly alone, confronting this welling sadness, I called home. My mother answered and a little voice escaped my body, "Hello."

"Who is this?" she said.

This unrecognizable voice again spoke through me, "It's Donna."

"Oh, Donna, you sound horrible ... that was probably not the right thing to say. What's wrong?"

The same sad little voice squeaked, "I just needed my mother." ... silence ...

Then I heard my mother crying.... "Your whole life, you never needed me. The others did. But from the time you walked, you never needed me. I wish you were here, so I could hug you. I wish you could be here for Christmas."

I walked at nine months. My mother was telling me that from the time I was nine months old, she did not mother me. She did not mother me in the way I so craved—because I wouldn't let her. Now that was sure an eye-opening message.

I began to reflect on my behavior and realized that often just when I needed affection and love, for some reason, I would push people away. Now what was that about? Sabotage at its best. Well, be assured, I have cleared that old, self-defeating pattern and am much more fulfilled because of this honest and enlightening conversation, which would never have occurred if I hadn't allowed the space for my mother to show up in her own authentic way.

Release people to be who they choose to be. Just as you would not walk in the garden and complain to the sunflower that you wished it was a daffodil, recognize and be grateful for the beauty in each individual. Celebrate the opportunity that you get to choose what people you "pick." Your good is never limited by your relationships, but instead should be enhanced by them.

> Piglet sidled up to Pooh from behind. "Pooh!" he whispered.
> "Yes, Piglet?"
> "Nothing," said Piglet, taking Pooh's paw.
> "I just wanted to be sure of you."
>
> ~ *A.A Milne*, The House at Pooh Corner

Circle of Appreciation

> The more you learn what to do with yourself, and the more
> you do for others, the more you will enjoy the abundant life.
>
> ~ William J.H. Boetcher

Our world sometimes seems to be focused on the negative. If a clerk is rude or gives bad service, a complaint is lodged with the manager, but how often do people fill out a comment card or let the manager know when they receive good service? Do you? And what about those you live with or interact with every day? How often do you voice what you like about them? What you appreciate about them? Letting a child know that something he did inspired you can be a valuable esteem builder. Telling your sister that you are impressed with the ways she puts colors together when decorating can provide a similar boost.

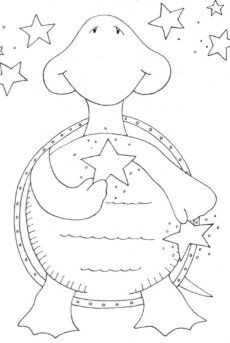

> Take every opportunity
> to reflect to another
> what you appreciate
> about them.
>
> ~ Turtle Wisdom

One lean Christmas, without the necessary funds for gifts, I made little stars on shiny paper and placed a small sticker in the center. I wrote one or two words on the sticker which sincerely expressed what I treasured about this person: "Expansion" for a brother going through much growth and "Humor" for a sister with remarkably quick wit. Without much hoopla I sent the little stars off in a package. My family responded with delight for me taking the time to appreciate them with such a heartfelt gift.

> A friend is someone who knows
> the song in your heart,
> and can sing it back to you
> when you have forgotten the words.
>
> ~ *Unknown*

In what ways can you create a "Circle of Appreciation?" Good words spread in greater and greater outreaching circles. Let the goodness multiply as you recognize what you appreciate and praise it.

Your belief in others can be surprisingly influential. You never know when something you say will be exactly what a person needs to hear in a moment of sadness or self-doubt. Your encouragement may be the one thing they need to hang onto or to move forward. Let your sincere thoughts of appreciation be expressed. Positive words are worth the time and effort to be spoken; compliments are never wasted. Faith in a person can be a powerful creative force. Think about who has impacted your life by noticing your value or giving you a kind word of encouragement. Make a difference to those around you— add a touch of sunshine to their day!

> When you like a flower, you just pluck it.
> But when you love a flower, you water it daily.
>
> ~ Buddha

Bodhisattva Lesson

In the Buddhist tradition there are stories of the bodhisattva, a being who has reached the gate of enlightenment, yet refuses to cross the threshold. She sees that there are many others who need help on this journey and so she remains on this side of the gate to help them cross over. Her path is one of mercy and compassion. These stories provide a poignant lesson that we are all in this lifetime together.

It is easy to see that others' actions affect us by looking at crime, terrorism, or world conflicts. Since this book was first published in 2005, we have sustained a world health emergency with the unprecedented pandemic in 2020-2023 and seen how faraway places can have a dramatic impact in our own backyard. Even on a smaller scale, moment by moment, interaction by interaction, we affect each other. In turn, the energy we create affects our collective vibrational environment.

How do you treat the cashier at the grocery store? In what way do you look at (or avoid looking at) the panhandler on the street corner? How do you respond to your child when he tugs at your shirt tails while you are making an important phone call? How well do you listen when a co-worker is sharing a disparaging experience? Observe your own behavior and refine it to genuinely reflect how you choose to treat others.

I am not suggesting that you premeditate every word you utter or become stilted in your behavior for fear of acting inappropriately. Yet, by examining and refining our behavior, we can relate in a more self-aligned manner. We can choose to act in ways which more fully embraces our true nature.

Most of us remember the classic Christmas story, *It's a Wonderful Life*, in which the main character, George, wishes he was never born. An angel shows him how dramatically life would be altered if he had not lived in his hometown, by showing him the ripple effect from his seemingly small actions which carried a much greater impact than he ever knew on those around him.

We all are an important piece of the mix. We help to hold the overall balance by what we do or what we do not do. By being more conscious of our thoughts, attitudes, and actions, we can affect others in the way we would best imagine or desire. For example, we must first find peace within ourselves, and share peace with those around us, if we ever hope to have peace in our greater world.

Understand and accept that what you do really does make a difference. When relating to others, your willingness to expose your soft belly through authentic relationships enriches our world. Seek out those who know and support you as you open to them in an authentic manner; share your deepest self with those you love.

12

Turtle Wisdom: She Who Holds Up the World

You may have been asking yourself, "Why the turtle?" I'll share the details of how *Turtle Wisdom* came into its name, but first, here's some information I discovered after the book had been published and was so well-received. I found out that "turtle" is loved and revered around the globe.

The turtle is an ancient symbol of feminine wisdom and strength. In China, the tortoise is regarded as one of the Four Spiritually Endowed (or Auspicious) Creatures, representing the North, Yin, and the element of Water—denoting strength, endurance, and longevity. Mythological turtles are thought to be strong, wise, and kind, and believed to be available to assist those going through transitions. And in many different cultures over thousands of years, the turtle has symbolized Mother Earth because she carries her home on her back.

The stories, myths, and symbolism of the Turtle are fascinating:

- In Hindu mythology, the world is held by four elephants standing on a giant turtle. She literally "holds up the world" on her back.
- In another Indian legend, we are told there is an endless stack of turtles supporting all of life, "turtles all the way down!"

- In another story told in several cultures, there are creatures (large and small) working together to build the earth on the turtle's back, recognizing turtle's ability to provide support, strength, and feminine wisdom by birthing the new world.
- In a Chinese myth a turtle became the world, which was his shell. The bottom flat part (the plastron) contained the ocean, and the upper dome (the carapace) formed the heavens. The four corners of the earth are on his feet.
- According to Greek legend, the tortoise could hatch its eggs just by looking at them.
- For Native Americans the thirteen cycles of the thirteen moons relates to the fertility of females. A new moon is born every 28 days. On a personal note, when I first wrote this book, the writing of it seemed to affect my typically consistent "moon time."
- Turtle is often held as a sign of fertility and associated with the power to heal female diseases including infertility. Fertile Turtle is an image of determinedness, patience, and the ability to navigate through challenges.
- In some cultures, Turtle is seen as the Eternal Mother, Divine Mother, or Womb of All.
- She is also recognized as Protector of Mature Wombs: one who turns into life through creative endeavors. Turtle stays with us as we age through all of life's stages.

Turtle Birth

What would happen if turtles held a giant rock concert on the beach? Certain species of migrating turtles meet with their extended families when it's their time to nest—coming together to "jam" in very large groups. The most spectacular is the mass nesting of Arribida, a ruddy sea turtle in Orissa, India. Up to 200,000 turtles nest on just three miles of beach within two days. The volume of reproductive output overwhelms their predators, with many nests hidden among the crowd, escaping detection, and assuring their survival. In the natural light the newly hatched sea turtles easily make their way to the safety of the sea, instinctively knowing how to find the water. We, too, know where to go by following the light.

> **How Do You Hold Up Your World?**
>
> How many expectations or responsibilities
> are you carrying on your back?
>
> How many roles do you fill every day?
> Some of us hit the ground running
> and never stop until we lay our heads to rest each night.
>
> The feminine principle is non-hierarchical
> and non-competitive, instead being inclusive and embracing.
> She gets ahead, not by stepping over others,
> but by rising with them.

Despite her significant and meaningful role, there is something delightfully playful about the turtle. Turtles swim, but they also float and free dive with ease and grace. Do you find life an ongoing struggle or a great adventure? Are you having fun with its twists and turns? You can strive to carry all you must do (as well as what you want to do) in a healthy and balanced manner—fulfilled, not frazzled by the busy life you lead. Remember to take time out to play, to refresh, and renew.

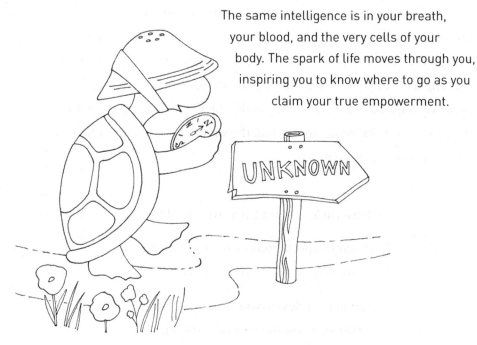

Nature's wisdom is remarkable. The same intelligence is in your breath, your blood, and the very cells of your body. The spark of life moves through you, inspiring you to know where to go as you claim your true empowerment.

Why "Turtle Wisdom?"

I have been asked many times, "Why did you call this book 'Turtle Wisdom?'" I didn't purposely choose it, but rather the turtle analogy came as an unexpected inspiration in a distinctively clear way that I've learned to notice and trust. It popped out of my mouth with no conscious decision to speak it and as I heard the words vibrate outside of me there was a strong remembrance and a resonance of unmistakable truth.

I am the oldest child in my family. My sister, Darcey, is the second of five. As often happens in families, my sister and I were very different growing up, each discovering our own special niche. We had a tendency to clash, and our personalities led us in very different directions as we grew into adulthood.

During her divorce from a long, tumultuous marriage, I reached out and offered support to Darcey. She had been left with very little except for her young daughter and a lot of bills. I told her how special she was, and that no matter what, she was taking away that which was most precious—herself. "You get you," I said. I think it was an especially sweet message coming from me.

A short time later, Darcey left a pivotal message in my voice mail. I saved it for many years! She said, "I am calling because I need to hear you say it. I tried telling myself, but no one says it like you, 'YOU GET YOU!'" she screamed into the phone. "You have to tell people about this. They need to hear it."

As I put the phone down from listing to this voice message, I spoke into the room with no one present, "You get You: Turtle Wisdom."

Then, "Turtle Wisdom, what's that?"

When I looked at the manuscript I had been writing at the request of my clients for a touchstone between sessions, it all made sense. That early title has evolved into *Turtle Wisdom: Coming Home to Yourself* and our turtle, Shelby T. Wisdom, has been embraced far and wide because of her universal significance and inspirational symbolism.

In mentioning my choice to use Turtle Wisdom as a focal point, I have described the process, which, for me, is the very best way these things develop. My creative inspirations often lead me in a new, unexpected direction. When I trust my inner guidance, I learn all I need to know. By exploring these synchronicities, I have developed an avenue for my inner yearnings. I am grateful for all they bring, for their scope is often much greater than I could possibly imagine.

Upon contemplation, I did find many reasons why knowing and appreciating yourself is turtle wisdom. Turtles carry most of what they need with them wherever they go. Females of some species can even store sperm, so they don't have to mate annually. You carry within you the knowledge and the wisdom to find everything you would need or want for your highest good. You either already have it or *you can go get it!* And your greatest resource is found by tapping into your Essential Core Self.

> The visual impression
> of the shell reminds us
> of our own ability to
> carry what is essential.
>
> *~ Turtle Wisdom*

The shell is also an appropriate symbol of self-contained safety, furthering our awareness that we are responsible for developing our own protection when it's needed.

> So successful was this protective armour
> that it became the cornerstone of turtle architecture.
>
> *~ Dr. Tim Halliday*

Safety and Protection

> Different lifestyles and ecologies have led to other alterations in the shell structure. Land turtles typically have high-vaulted shells as a defense against their predators crushing jaws. Water turtles have lower, more streamlined shells that offer less water resistance during swimming. Extreme flattening is found among soft shells, helping them to hide beneath sand and mud on the bottom of their watery habitat.
>
> *~ Dr. Tim Halliday*

My favorite is the flat Pancake Turtle, which crawls into a small crevice between two rocks and then puffs up its shell by filling its lungs with air so his body is stuck, and the predator cannot remove him. Brilliant! This clever adaptation is just one of many found within the more than 350 species of turtles.

In fact, adaptability is a common turtle trait. Being ectothermic, they seek shelter under logs when it is hot and sit in the sun when it is cool. They can carry water with them or lie dormant until rain brings life-sustaining moisture.

> The commonly held notion of a turtle shell conjures the image of a very rounded top, dependable and sturdy. What better place to envision our womb of consciousness, where we can dream our dreams and from which we can birth our reality?
>
> *~ Turtle Wisdom*

How Adaptable are You?

Are you investing in the happenings of your day playing out exactly as you have planned? How open are you to a spontaneous, unexpected turn of events?

- Structure can help us to be productive, but are you flexible about the way in which your to-do lists get done?
- Do you work hard at shaping your recreational time, putting forth a lot of effort just to have fun?"
- Do you strive to be perfect for your job, for your family, for yourself? Are you straightening the couch cushions even when no one is looking?!?

> Can you enjoy the present moment or are you somewhere else strategizing what is to come? Are you the life planner who sets forth a decree and then pushes, cajoles, and forces the lines of that particular picture. When you are rigidly focused on how things unfold, determined to mold people and events into a specific idea of how it "should be," you limit life's great potential.

By identifying what is truly important to you and releasing the minor details, you allow a much broader range of experience. Often what develops may be sweeter or grander than what you could have ever imagined.

Instead of trying to squeeze your life into neat little boxes all tied up with pretty bows, open to the world as your playground and look far beyond into the horizon. You will not be limited by what is in front of you, not focused only on what you can see.

It is actually the details of how your goals come to pass that you might consider surrendering. You can plant roses, but if you stand by their side and try to peel each petal down in your determined timetable, you destroy something beautiful. If you plant those roses and then sit back and watch with delight as they open in their perfect time and manner, you can then behold their rich, natural beauty. When you let go of forcing things to be as you imagine they should be, you allow them the time and the space to evolve freely.

> Embrace the opportunity of what might be: envision what is possible, set your intention, and then let it go, without allowing any myopic view to limit its scope.

Happiness is like a butterfly, the more you chase it, the more it eludes you. But if you turn your attention to other things, it comes and sits softly on your shoulder.

~ Henry David Thoreau

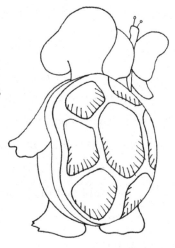

Longevity and Diversity

Turtles were here when the dinosaurs walked the earth millions of years ago. And they are quite diverse: some species have short life spans, while others can live up to 150 years. The endangered bog turtle is only three to four and a half inches long, while the leather back turtle can be up to eight feet long and weigh over 1500 pounds. Some are vegetarian and others are not. Turtles can be smelly, such as the Southern Loggerhead Musk Turtle. And there are many variations in the markings of their shells, including some that are exquisitely designed, such as the radiated tortoise of Madagascar with its brilliant yellow, sunburst mountainous carapace, surrounded by a delightfully fringed border. Turtle is a symbol of diversity, sustainability, and longevity.

> Many turtle species carry growth records along with them on their horny scutes ... much like an annual ring on a tree trunk.
>
> ~ Dr. Tim Halliday

We, too, carry our history with us! Seen or unseen—with obvious patterned markings or invisible strokes—our past follows us down the path wherever we go. That's why coming to terms with it, gleaning its value, and making peace with it is so essential.

In Native American teaching, the turtle is the oldest symbol on our planet. As the eternal Mother, she is our origin, and our lives evolve from her. She is necessary for our survival.

Regardless of your beliefs about how you were created, you were born into the womb of the earth and when you die, the ashes of your body return to the earth. It is from this place of respect and connection to our Earth Mother that we recognize the symbolic importance of Turtle, for she can remind us of our kinship with the sacred rhythms of nature and the original blueprint embedded in the seed of our souls. All creatures have their own unique and precious connection with life. Every plant, every animal, every insect, and every winged has something significant to share. We can enrich our experience by learning from theirs much like the opportunity found in knowing other humans! The world is rich with diversity in culture and characters; opening to those who are different from us can expand our limited scope and reveal new horizons.

One with Nature

> When one tugs at a single thing in nature,
> he finds it attached to the rest of the world.
>
> ~ John Muir

On holiday in Nuevo Vallarta, walking along the beach, with my feet on the wet sand and waves lapping around my shins, I became lost in that precious space of no thought, only pure appreciation for the moment and being acutely aware of the sensations of sand and water against my skin. I gazed periodically down at my feet, out past the immediate waves to the horizon, and just ahead of me down the beach. I noticed a little girl about four or five in a sweet blue dress with little white flowers. She was taking a walk with her mother and brothers, looking for treasures along the water's edge. What I distinctly noticed about this little girl was how sure-footed she was. There were other kids, and adults, too, for that matter, who walked with feet used to being held within protective shoes. They stepped gingerly with an uncertain stride that hardly touched the ground, intent on getting to where they were going and certainly not taking the time to pause there.

This little girl was different. Her chest was puffed out in front of her leading the way and her feet came down with a determined force, taking step after step until something caused her to pause and inspect a new discovery. She seemed very used to the beach, akin to nature, and at home bare-footed, as she romped freely within this delightful playground. Then, I noticed that mama walked the same way; daughter had learned to love the land from mama; this appreciation was ingrained.

Later, I saw the little girl swimming in the shallow waves, and she still wore that sweet blue dress with the little white flowers on it. She giggled and romped with ease and familiarity as she bobbed up and down in the ocean water. I delighted in her resonance with the natural world and her ability to be joyful in the simplicity of the day. Seeing her reminded me of how I loved the beach as a child—although I don't know if I was ever that comfortable in the sand and surf.

In the present time, I soaked in the sensation of sand between my toes and water against my skin, letting those sensations penetrate to my core. Ah! My wave walk nurtured a very deep part of me in more ways than I can even say.

Turtle Birth

In the interconnection of all of life, we do have a privilege and a responsibility to look out for others. When we apply this consciousness of wholeness to how we show up as a part of the natural world, we can make changes based on caring and consideration. We are Earth Guardians ... and as such, we touch her and her creatures gently.

One balmy summer night under the full moon, I midwifed a turtle giving birth. The giant sea turtle was part of a protection program on Isla Mujeres, Mexico. I facilitated retreats to this magical island for six years and this birthing experience was one of my most memorable moments.

It was close to midnight when we crossed the gate and walked along the welcoming beach. The turtle has already climbed out of the ocean to dig a womb in the sand. She was methodical in her movements and kept going without pause until the very deep hole was dug. She then positioned herself within this cozy inlet as she was clearly in active labor. Her grunts and sighs were similar to a human giving birth. We watched and waited.

I was poised at her tail, and after a short time, "plunk," out came a warm, ooze-covered egg, plopping right into my waiting palm. I cradled my other hand on top, gently but surely holding this treasure. I marveled at the sense of new life, warm and vibrant between my hands.

Suddenly with great force, I was showered with sand. "You better move, or you'll be buried," our Mexican friend told me. The mother was covering her egg (and me!) for safety. These turtles are endangered, so the "baby" egg was placed in a pail and transported to the fenced nursery where it would be safe from predators. There it would hatch and grow until it was big enough to survive. Then it would be released to the sea.

> There are times when we, too, are like endangered babies who need a gentle hand and a safe place to grow. It is never too late to draw in the support and encouragement you need to help you become the person you can be.
>
> Who could help midwife a part of your birth?
> Reach out to those who can help nurture your evolving self.
> Trust and believe in the perfection of your process.

In order to have faith, we must have a conviction
that all is well. In order to keep faith,
we must allow nothing to enter our thought
which will weaken this conviction.

~ Ernest Holmes

I live with the conviction that there is an ever expanding and evolving goodness in my life. Today is today, and tomorrow is tomorrow. I live passionately in the presence of today and refuse to be wrapped up in worries of the future. I believe in my capacity to draw toward me the people and situations I desire to positively impact my life. I surrender daily to an assurance and anticipation of what is now coming forth. And I claim my good.

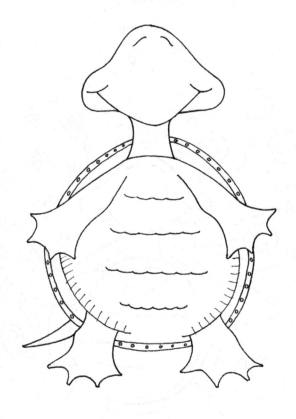

Make conscious choices.
Be fully alive!

13

Open to Possibilities

What progress, you ask, have I made?
I have begun to be a friend to myself.

~ Hecato, Greek Philosopher

Hopefully, the time has come when you can greet yourself arriving at your door and see the reflection that is your own looking right back at you ... and delight in your own face. You smile with a warm welcome and offer a cozy chair. You can look upon this one with acceptance, perhaps even admiration, as you have come to intimately know and like her. No longer a stranger held at bay, but rather your greatest ally, the one who follows you day by day.

She knows your heart and your soul. She sees you. And it is good.

Tell me, what is it you plan to do with your one wild and precious life?

~ Mary Oliver

It's been said before and it bears repeating, "We are the people we've been waiting for." We each have our experiences with all their potential. We each have the ability to live life in the very best way for our individualized self. You are the person you've been waiting for. And if you can look at your journey as evolving those essential parts that are needed to reveal your authenticity, if you can grab a hold of the responsibility to change and refine what is necessary, then you can honestly say, "Yeah! Thank goodness I am who I am." How exciting it is to be "you" this time around. Yeeha! Reveal the nuances of your self-realized nature; become the person you were meant to be.

And you can also question, "What is mine to do? And what is not mine to do?" There is just so much space in a lifetime. What do you need to let go of? And what are the things that are really yours to embrace and live by? Have the courage to say, "Yes. This is it. This is mine!"

Take note when a little voice surfaces that whimpers, "Who, me?" I believe that insecurity is somewhat of a universal challenge. I work with writers to help them open their writing channels and get their books published. I find it very common, almost without exception, that they ask this question in some shape or form. "Who am I to do this?" The question has been asked by many who are recognized as experts in their field, respected and honored for their knowledge and yet the doubt still surfaces. "Who am I to write this book?"

I like to respond with "who are you not to write that book?" shifting the consideration to "if you don't do it, what about the people who could benefit from that book? They won't get to read it because you didn't write it."

This is true about what you are inspired to do, too. Because if you shift your focus to what you want to do and the importance of that project, it's no longer tapping into those "not good enough," "not worthy enough," "who the heck am I" kind of universal doubts that we seem to carry. You can consider the project on its merits alone. Remember that Thomas Edison said, "if we did all the things we are capable of, we would literally astound ourselves."

> There is more
> to you than even
> you know.
>
> ~ Turtle Wisdom

> I cannot do all the good that the world needs.
> But the world needs all the good that I can do.
>
> ~ Jana Stanfied

Right when I was trying to summon the courage to release a book that shared thorny personal details as a part of my work on trauma and healing, inspirational musician, Jana Stanfield, came to town and sang her motivational song on the platform right in front of me.

"I cannot do all the good that the world needs. But the world needs all the good I can do ...." Also true—you cannot do all the good that the world needs, but the world needs all the good you can do. And we cannot do all the good that the world needs, but the world needs all the good we can do.

Cynthia James, a passionate and dedicated new thought leader, was on the stage at the same time. I've known Cynthia for years and she was aware of my struggle with this pivotal book release. At the time I was questioning if I should put the manuscript away in a chest with notes to publish it after my death. Synchronizing with the particularly impactful words, "I cannot do all the good that the world needs, but the world needs all the good that I can do," Cynthia pointed her finger at me from that elevated stage and then motioned a book appearing in front of her, which she opened in the next motion. She did this several times when that potent line was sung. Again and again, she demonstrated the book being put out in the world. I got the message ... and *8 Keys to Wholeness: Tools for Hope-Filled Healing* went to press. It is now award-winning and internationally published.

What is the "good" that the world needs that you can do? Be brave. And share it.

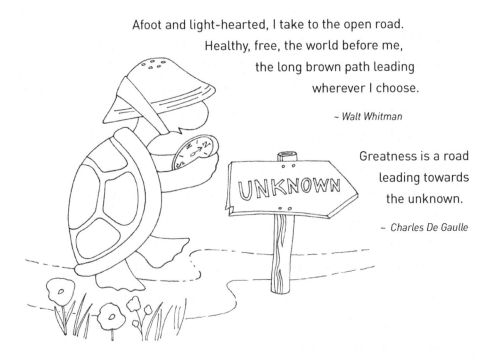

Afoot and light-hearted, I take to the open road.
Healthy, free, the world before me,
the long brown path leading
wherever I choose.

~ Walt Whitman

Greatness is a road leading towards the unknown.

~ Charles De Gaulle

Sometimes we fear failure, but other times we fear success. More often than you might think, people will sabotage their accomplishments right before they come to fruition. Have you ever noticed someone who worked for years toward a goal and then, just before achieving it, suddenly switched directions and missed the mark? In the areas of physical, mental, or emotional healing, this might happen when someone is not yet ready—perhaps there is still a nuance to be experienced or an important understanding to be revealed.

Succeeding can also make you visible in a way that you fear. It exposes you somehow—you are out there, vulnerable, in the sharing of your innermost self. If this resonates with you, you might want to revisit Exposing Your Soft Belly (chapter 11, page 183).

> Our deepest fear is not that we are inadequate.
> Our deepest fear is that we are
> powerful beyond measure.
> It is our light, not our darkness,
> that most frightens us ...
> Your playing small doesn't serve the world.
> There's nothing enlightened about shrinking
> so that other people won't feel insecure around you ...
> And as we let our own light shine,
> we unconsciously give other people
> permission to do the same ...
> As we're liberated from our own fear,
> our presence automatically liberates others.
>
> ~ Marianne Williamson

Why were we born?
We are here on this earth
to experience the fullness,
the sweetness of life
with all it has to offer.
Imagine the possibilities!
Right now,
regardless of what is or is not
happening in your life,
where could you go from here?

~Turtle Wisdom

Your most evolved self is "calling you." It is beckoning you to become all that you can be. There is not one specific role or destiny you must live out, but rather a vast array of potential possibilities for you to explore and express your true self. While your innermost core pushes you to gift the world with your unique talents, you alone guide your path because you have the freedom to choose what direction that expression takes. We all need your contribution. What you have to offer is not exactly like anyone else's part. As puzzle pieces connect to form a beautiful image, many souls unite for the good of our planetary evolution.

What would life be like if you lived from this inner core connection and conviction, living your potential moment by moment? What if your thoughts, words, and actions were conscious ones, embracing the life you were given? Life is an incredible opportunity to bring forth your greatest creation. Be delighted to share yourself with the world. Be invested in how you are living and adjust when necessary to remain aligned with your truest expression. Every moment has significance. Every contribution affects the whole.

> Making choices is the most powerful thing
> that you do in your life. Choices liberate, and they imprison.
> They create illness and they create health. They shape
> your life … Each choice creates a future. It brings
> into being one of the many possible futures.
> That is the future you will live in.
>
> ~ Gary Zukov

Develop a faith that urges you to step out in ways your inner being longs to express. Take a chance. Experiment. What have you got to lose? Explore new ideas … Pursue your dreams. When all is said and done, do you want to come to the end of your life with doubts about what you could have tried? About the parts not yet lived? Or would you rather live life with zest and eager participation, choosing your focus consciously and knowing that whatever the outcome, your life is your own?

You are doing it your way!

Awaken with the promise of each day, as you recognize the true gift of life and your potential for unwrapping the many layers of who you are and what you have to experience. Enrich your relationships as you authentically interact, sharing the expression of your inner beauty. Be fully alive!

Savor this human existence and by doing so you will elevate it to even more of what it can be.

Set your sights beyond what
you can easily reach
and you will easily reach
beyond what you
can imagine.

~ *Anonymous*

Namasté

That which is perfect
and Divine in me
sees that which is perfect
and Divine in you.

Postscript

You Write
The Final Chapter(s)

Well, there you have it! It began with you, and it ends with you. For in life, it does truly begin and end with you.

At this point in our journey together, it is my hope that you have a deeper, sweeter, perhaps even expanded sense of appreciation for that unique and precious person who is "You." There is no one else exactly like you. And there is a contribution to our world only you can make—regardless of how small you think your actions are, remember they do matter. Moment by moment, piece by piece, your actions have an impact. The vibration of your actions ripple out and affects the rest of us ... and the greater world.

There is no way to escape yourself. And there is no way to escape your connection with everything else. The paradox is that as much as you are always independently and uniquely you, you are also interdependently connected to the grand "We." And even if you never meet a particular individual, in some way your word, your action, your attitude, or belief may vibrate outward, reaching and affecting the balance in a way that touches that unknown stranger.

So be aware. Be conscious in how you choose to live and make the best choices to be the "you" that You wish to be.

For the reality is you are the author who has written all your chapters, and you will write all the final chapters, too.

I look forward to seeing what you create!

Self-Realized Turtle

The End/The Beginning

Author's Note

As I lay these words before you, it is the last full moon of the summer, 2023. The rare Blue Supermoon smiles upon the fruition of my heartfelt endeavor. *Turtle Wisdom* has been with me for a long time, often leading the way with unexpected twists and turns. She has provided delightful opportunities to find friends I might otherwise not meet. Sitting in a hot tub in Sedona, Arizona, I am asked to share who I am and when I mention my first book a woman starts weeping, "That book changed my life," she said. And another who called to thank me for the acceptance and encouragement she found within my pages, became a student taking every workshop I offered, and eventually grew to be a lifelong friend. Gee, I even visited a bank branch where I was unknown to the tellers, hoping to cash a check. After I found myself without the necessary ID, I asked the branch manager if there was any other way. I knew they had my signature on file. He agreed but said, "Do you have something with your name and picture on it?" "Yes, I do," and I dashed to the car to grab one of my books. When I showed it to him, he turned it over and over, staring at it intently. "This is you?" "Yes." "Well, right now I'm reading this book! It lives on my night table. Of course, we can cash your check." I *love* those stories. I hold dear a stunning rainbow of stories, warm glows of every hue ... I feel a special connection with everyone in them.

This eighteen-year anniversary rewrite has taken much longer than anticipated—a full nine months of creativity, attention, and care. From the little glimmers of ideas surfacing in my mind's eye to the word-by-word detailed scrutiny, to tenderly sculpt this baby into her rightful birth. I offer her to you with love and the best intention. May she touch you as she has so many others. May she free your heart and draw forth the essence of your soul to reveal the magnificence of who you truly are.

With love and blessings,

Donna

Unpack the Shell ...
Take "Turtle Wisdom" Along on Your Journey.

Throughout this book, we've left a purposeful trail of Turtle Wisdom quotes—inspirational, motivational, and encouraging. Precious reminders of who you are and what lives inside of you. In times of need or when you just want a boost, skim through the pages to find one of the little turtles with Turtle Wisdom quotes on top and unpack that shell.

1. Read the quote. Let it dance in your mind.

2. Read it again, perhaps this time out loud. Notice how it feels inside your body.

3. Copy the quote onto an index card or notepad.

4. Now carry it with you today and observe how many times it seems relevant; notice when it speaks to you from your backpack or your purse.

5. If you take along our little turtle, Shelby T. Wisdom, and her words of wisdom, she is guaranteed to uplift your day.

Author and Illustrator

Donna DeNomme has cherished a lifetime dedicated to helping people claim their true voice. She invites us to recognize all facets of who we are, including the weaker or wounded parts so we might nurture them to heal and grow into their fullest potential. With an eclectic training in traditional and depth psychology, as well as alternative and indigenous practices, Donna is a conscious energy teacher, shamanic healer, ceremonial leader, and self-realization coach serving the community since 1987. She is also a Practitioner Emeritus for 32 years through the Centers for Spiritual Living.

Donna was recognized as Colorado's "Spiritual Health Guru" by *5280 Magazine* for her innovative empowerment techniques which inspire you to claim "Your Wisdom Story," so you can consciously compose your next chapter, reveal your authentic self, and design the life you desire.

She is the award-winning, internationally published author of seven books, two meditation CD's, and several online programs including *A Write of Passage* and *8 Essential Keys: Tools for Hope-Filled Healing and Expansive Evolutionary Growth.* www.YourWisdomStory.com

Susan Andra Lion is an award-winning designer, author, and illustrator, the owner of a successful graphic design company, Sue Lion : ink. Her career has a broad client base, including for-profit corporations and not-for-profit entities. She has written and illustrated many adult and children's books, and has a full line of illustrations that honor Mother Earth. www.suelion.com

Confidence-Building and Transformation Tools
Award-Winning Books/Cards by Donna DeNomme

Turtle Wisdom: Coming Home to Yourself
This popular, internationally published confidence-building companion, first released in 2005 is now in its 3rd edition. The 18-year anniversary book has grown from 120 pages to 256 pages with new stories, contemplations, and practical wisdom.

Turtle Wisdom Personal Illumination Cards
A complete confidence-building program in a box! These inspirational cards cultivate personal trust, a belief in the overall goodness of life, and acceptance of your precious, evolving self. Shared by those young and old.

Turtle Wisdom Playbook
A Motivational Coloring Adventure leads to your beautiful, magnificent Self.
Coloring + Activities = Super Fun!

Ophelia's Oracle: Discovering the Healthy, Happy, Self-Aware, and Confident Girl in the Mirror
Co-authored with Tina Proctor
15 national and international awards for excellence, *Ophelia's Oracle* embraces readers with a dramatic, full-color design featuring a story girls love, fun activities, interviews, illustrations, and poetry. For girls 8-12 and women love it, too.

8 Keys to Wholeness: Tools for Hope-Filled Healing

An invitation to heal so we may transform our personal and collective realities. Having sustained brutal emotional, sexual, and ritual abuse as a child, Donna reminds us that the ultimate truth is not found in our wounding, but rather in the discovery of how we can heal those wounds. She understands healing is a sometimes difficult, yet revolutionary path that reveals our truest, essential Self. Offering practical insights from over thirty years as a spiritual teacher, conscious energy healer, shamanic facilitator, and self-realization coach, she introduces a potent triad of chakras to help us access strength and resilience, so we may create true and lasting healing.

As You Feel, So You Heal: A Write of Passage

Look at your emotions with curiosity and a new whole world of insight opens up. This book leads you through the delightful journey of sacred writing as a means for self-discovery, healing and transformation, celebrating all of life, and appreciating the unique gifts you have to offer. Whether you make your way through this "Write of Passage" with pen and paper or simply consider the questions, meditations, and processes in thoughtful contemplation, you'll gain a deeper appreciation of your beloved authentic self. Recognized for excellence with the prestigious Benjamin Franklin Gold Award, the acclaimed Nautilus Silver Award, and the COVR Visionary Silver Award.

Guided Imagery Meditation: Spinning the Light

Elevate energies within you to their highest and best vibratory level. Consciously in-light-en our world.

Guided Meditation Reiki : Sacred Journey

This guided imagery CD supports you with "A Symbol Awakening" and "A Symbol Deepening."

Opportunities to Work with Donna

Writing is an act of discovery. Whether you write for your own benefit or to share with others, when you explore the vast contours and deep crevices, writing accesses information often just beyond your reach. It is there you find rich, organic material for your growth. At times, you may encounter a chaos of sorts, while at other times, a surprising new order. Like a rafter navigating treacherous rapids or a hiker meandering on a meditative path, the trail is not a defined one, but simply a discovery, step-by-step of reaching deeply within.

Write of Passage online / on demand
This dynamic online group includes presentations and focusing tools to stimulate creativity and your ability to access your own deeply delightful in-sight. Give yourself permission to explore writing as an enrichment practice for self-awareness, healing, transformation, and personal growth. We'll explore five potent gateways for self-discovery.

An easy-to-follow program in the convenience of your own home, filled with bite-size video sessions with engaging stories, guided meditations, stimulating contemplative prompts, and practical instruction to open up your transformational writing. Go through this program at your own pace for optimum value.

Heart & Soul Reflections
A Guided Writing Immersion held in the Meditation Garden
Not just for writers. Find your own wise voice as you move through a transformational process that opens the mind and unlocks your soul for accessing your deepest insight and wisdom. What do you have to say through the writing? What does your writing want to say to you? Let's explore through guided practices and a welcomed time to refresh and renew.

Write just for you. Or write to share far and wide. Come with no idea of where your writing will take you or bring along a project you're presently working on—develop that project that's been sitting on the shelf or being held captive in a computer file.

30 Day Invitation: Coming Home to Yourself
A comforting, encouraging, and delightfully expansive 30-day adventure to discover, accept, appreciate, transform, and skillfully craft your most important relationship. Awaken a masterful life, one of your very own design. More than a coaching program, more than a class, more than a workshop series—and yet a bit of each. Our committed 30-day group helps you to be more, have more. Why? Because you can!

Your Wisdom Story
You are a Masterpiece. Your most evolved self is "calling you." It is beckoning you to become all that you can be. Imagine the possibilities!

Your Wisdom Story is written through everything you experience—from your past, your present, and your future. There are vast nuances, a beautiful display of color, light and shadow. In this three-part series you will purposefully shape the life you desire as you claim the brilliance of your own wisdom story. Set your sights beyond what you can easily reach and you will easily reach beyond what you can imagine.

More Opportunities to Work with Donna

8 Essential Keys: Tools for Hope-Filled Healing and Expansive Evolutionary Growth
What can change in eight short weeks? A Lot! More than self-help, this program is about self-fulfillment. Heal your deepest wounds through a comprehensive system that engages the mind, comforts the emotions, and utilizes the energetic systems of the body to bring forth true and lasting results. Tap into your heart's desires and your soul's longings ... as you accept your Divine Inheritance, bring forward your Divine Passion, and manifest your Divine Mission.

Bonus "Get-You-Started" Week + Companion Book + Reference Card + One private coaching session + 8 optional Online Weekly Meetings

Lightworkers Legacy: The Heroine's Journey
We are being called to show up more authentically, to find our full voice, and to embrace our wildest dreams and sweetest happiness. A committed virtual series. Power boost your evolutionary growth.

Private Sessions and VIP Mastery
Donna has a small number of private sessions available as well as full 4–6 hour VIP Mastery dates. To request a phone call to determine if one of those spots is yours, email: donna@YourWisdomStory.com.

To be added to our email newsletter list, register on our website, www.YourWisdomStory.com. Choose the "special people" list to include Colorado-based events or the "Online Programs & Retreats" for only our virtual offerings.

Support your turtle and ocean conservation non-profits.
Thirteen days of free inspirational videos leading up to World Turtle Day are available on YouTube. To subscribe to our channel, go to: www.youtube.com/@donnadenomme4430/videos

Made in the USA
Las Vegas, NV
02 December 2024